# CITYSPOTS
# PALER

**Fran Folsom**

**Written and photographed by Fran Folsom**
Front cover photograph copyright Alamy Images

**Produced by 183 Books**
Design/layout/maps: Chris Lane and Lee Biggadike
Editorial/project management: Stephen York

**Published by Thomas Cook Publishing**
A division of Thomas Cook Tour Operations Limited
PO Box 227, Units 15/16, Coningsby Road,
Peterborough PE3 8SB, United Kingdom
email: books@thomascook.com
www.thomascookpublishing.com
+44 (0) 1733 416477

**First edition © 2006 Thomas Cook Publishing**
Text © 2006 Thomas Cook Publishing
Maps © 2006 Thomas Cook Publishing
ISBN-13: 978-1-84157-591-9
ISBN-10: 1-84157-591-7
Project Editor: Kelly Anne Pipes
Production/DTP: Steven Collins

Printed and bound in Spain by GraphyCems

# CONTENTS

## SYMBOLS & ABBREVIATIONS

The following symbols are used throughout this book:

| | | | |
|---|---|---|---|
| ☎ telephone | 🖷 fax | ✉ email | ⓦ website address |
| ⓐ address | 🕐 opening times | Ⓝ public transport connections |

The following symbols are used on the maps:

🛈  Tourist Information Office
✈  Airport

Hotels and restaurants are graded by approximate price as follows:
**€** budget price  **€€** mid-range price  **€€€** expensive
**€€€+** very expensive

## 24-HOUR CLOCK

All times in this book are given in the 24-hour clock system used
widely in Europe and in most international transport timetables.

◐ *Of all Palermo's ecclesiastical buildings, the cathedral is the most imposing*

# Introduction

There is an Italian saying 'The mystique of Palermo lingers with you forever'. In a gorgeous bay underneath the hulking Monte Pellegrino and fronting the wide and fertile Conca d'Oro (Golden Shell) valley, Palermo is magnificently sited.

This is a city of multi-layered history, starting with its founding as a Phoenician colony. It was taken by the Carthaginians in the fifth century, then came the Greeks, and in 254BC it was conquered by the Romans. Palermo's most glorious time came in AD831 when it was captured by the Arabs, under whose rule it blossomed as an Islamic cultural and intellectual centre. Two centuries later, under the Normans, Palermo was Europe's greatest metropolis.

By way of contrast, the 20th century was one of social and economic decline for the city. Allied bombs during World War II destroyed much of the port area and over seventy of the city's historic churches, today major restorations are ongoing at a painstakingly slow pace.

There is no other city in Italy quite like Palermo. On the cusp of a new beginning, it also celebrates its diverse history. Visiting here is thrilling for what the city has to offer, but, it can also be a challenge. Traffic is horrible as cars, trucks and buses clog the narrow streets, often coming to a complete standstill for hours. This has caused a yellow cloud of pollution to hang constantly over the city making air quality less than desirable, covering cars and buildings with dust.

In the year 2000 Palermo's Via Roma registered a higher level of air pollution than any other main street in Italy. City officials are working to put restrictions into place that will allow driving into Palermo only on certain days of the week. This is a city best seen on foot or by bicycle. Be careful, traffic not withstanding, Palermitans drive fast and stop for nothing that gets in their way.

Unlike many other large European cities you'll not see beggars or homeless people in the streets. What is commonplace though is petty crime – you would be well advised to avoid the markets and back street areas after dark, and don't flash around large amounts of money.

Most areas are safe in the daytime and nothing should stop you from enjoying the city. Vestiges from the 9th to the 12th century are abundant. But, it's the re-creation of the city between the 16th and 17th centuries that gave Palermo the appearance it has today: a straightforward grid pattern, jumbled by the prior existence of an Eastern beginning, and the destruction from World War II bombs.

Palermo's churches have always been richly endowed, either by wealthy families or monastic orders, and so visitors flock to them; from the Cattedrale to the richly coloured mosaics of Cappella Palatina inside the Royal Apartments, to the Norman built La Martorana. Along with these are many fine examples of baroque architecture such as San Giuseppe dei Teatini and Santa Caterina. To see Palermo from an architectural point of view means that you could miss its three excellent museums, the festivals and marketplaces, the puppet theatre and a plethora of outstanding restaurants.

Despite all this, Palermo is a jewel of the Mediterranean. No visit to Sicily would be complete without a stop in Palermo, where you will come not just to know the island, but to understand it.

# When to go

## SEASONS & CLIMATE

The best months for warm but not hot weather are May, June and September with October and November pleasant for hiking and swimming. Summer brings blistering heat blown in by the sirocco wind from North Africa. This season also brings thousands of visitors, limited hotel availability in the resort areas such as Mondello, and higher prices.

During December and January Palermo is damp, cold and rainy, making a heavy coat and umbrella necessary.

Spring arrives early, in February, when the almond trees blossom, this is the best time of year to visit. The Holy Week events leading up to Easter are spectacular, but, as you can imagine, crowded.

## ANNUAL EVENTS

### January

**Orthodox Epiphany** (6 January). Procession at Piana degli Albanesi, traditional costumes and the passing out of oranges.

### February

**Baroque Carnival** Centuries ago the aristocracy of Palermo would show off their wealth with lavish masked balls and parades throughout the city. Today the pre-Lent carnival is a citywide celebration of Palermo and its history. For a schedule of events contact the tourist office (❶ 091.605.8351).

### March

**Fiesta of San Giuseppe (St Joseph)** 19 March. Held in the old quarter of Palermo, Palermitans celebrate the life of the saint by preparing large

Patron saint Santa Rosalia is commemorated in a major festival

spreads of food. The food is reserved for 'members of the Holy family' portrayed by costumed parishioners, or the poor, or unmarried people. Taking part in the meal is known as *fari I virginieddi*.

**Easter**
Easter is celebrated with religious processions highlighting the last days of Christ's life. The *Cocchieri* (coachmen) procession on Good

Friday has costumed participants carrying the statues of the Madonna and Christ all over the city from the Chiesa della Madonna dell'Itria. The Good Friday *Procession dei Mistri* in Monreale (see page 114) where townspeople dress in traditional costume for Holy Week, is not to be missed. Brotherhoods of men, wearing blue satin hoods over their faces, carry crosses and the statue of the Madonna from the Duomo throughout the hilly streets of the village. Details are available from the tourist office.

## April
**St George's Day** (23 April) is celebrated with a procession at Piana degli Albanesi.
**Annual Windsurfing Festival** at Mondello. International competition.

## June
**KalsArt Festival** The start of the festival of live music, theatre and cinema events that takes place in the La Kalsa district. Runs from Mid-June–mid-Sept.

## July
**Festival of St Rosalia** (15 July). Commemorates the patron saint of Palermo who saved the city from the plague. Six days of processions and celebrations end with fireworks over the harbour.

## August
**Feast of the Assumption** or *ferragosto*, (15 August). An island-wide celebration capped off with fireworks.
**Il Palio dei Normanni** (13–14 August 2006). Medieval pageants and jousting contests in Piazza Armerina.

**PUBLIC HOLIDAYS**

**New Year's Day** 1 Jan
**Epiphany** 6 Jan
**Easter Monday** Mar/Apr
**Easter Sunday** Mar/Apr
**Liberation Day** 25 Apr
**Labour Day** 1 May
**Feast of St Rosalia** 15 July
**Feast of the Assumption** 15 Aug
**Feast of the Immaculate Conception** 8 Dec
**Christmas Day** 25 Dec
**St Stephen's Day** 26 Dec

**September**
**Pilgrimage to Monte Pellegrino** (4 September) to honour Saint Rosalia.

**September–December**
**Festival of Sacred Music.** At weekends in Monreale's churches (see page 123).

**November**
**Festival of the Dead** (2 November). Halloween-like celebrations, as deceased relatives are believed to return and leave gifts for children.

**December**
**Feast of the Immaculate Conception** 8 December. A holy day when statues of Mary are honoured around the city.

# The Mafia

*The Mafia is oppression, arrogance, greed, self-enrichment, power and hegemony above and against all other. It is not an abstract concept, or a state of mind, or a literary term... It is a criminal organization regulated by unwritten but iron and inexorable rules... The myth of a courageous and generous 'man of honor' must be destroyed, because a Mafioso is just the opposite.*

Cesare Terranova, Italian Magistrate, murdered in 1979

Palermo's wealth of culture – and that of Sicily in general – has been overshadowed by the region's history with the mob. Media and entertainment have turned Sicily into a worldwide metaphor for violence and organised crime. Mario Puzo's novel *The Godfather* rocked the country and was later adapted into an Academy Award-winning film that became the first part of a trilogy.

The Mafia (or *Cosa Nostra*) today is a symptom of the country's endemic political corruption, a phenomenon which has only worsened. In recent years it has been openly acknowledged that a large part of the funds pouring into Sicily from Rome and the European Union, ostensibly to redevelopment and restore Palermo's city centre and other areas of Sicily, are unaccounted for, channelled to dubious businessmen, or simply gone into the coffers of noted Mafia leaders.

The subtle control exerted by the Mafia is typically hidden, but, occasionally it does erupt in the news. In more recent times Mafia issues have maintained a high profile, following the instigation of the struggle to reassert the state's authority in the wake of a number of asassinations of anti-Mafia crusaders: Giovanni Falcone, who, in 1992, with his wife and three bodyguards, was blown up by a half ton of TNT on his way into Palermo from the airport. Two months later his colleague Paolo Borsellino and five of his bodyguards were victims of a car-bomb in Palermo. These were two of Palermo's most visible judges who refused to be intimidated by death threats routinely made against anti-Mafia investigators. Since then, the arrest of leading Mafia figures, starting with the arrest of the *capo dei capi* Salvatore Raiina in 1993, has seen the tide turning against the *Cosa Nostra*, helped by the testimony of many informers.

However, the problem is deeply rooted and unlikely to disappear completely, despite the efforts of various individuals. The leader among these is Leoluca Orlando, mayor of Palermo from 1993 to 2001, whose policy was to fight corruption at the municipal level by removing companies with links to organised crime from the tenders list of new contracts. Despite reversals, including disavowal by his own Christian Democrat party, Orlando has continued his fight at a national level, at the head of his own *Rete* (National) party.

Fortunately, for the casual traveller, the Mafia has little relevance, and the closest you will get to it is through the headlines in the local newspapers. Having said that, it is the cinematic portrayal of the Cosa Nostra in *The Godfather* trilogy that actually draws some travellers to Sicily in the hope of visiting locations that appear in the films. Most of the action that was actually shot on the island was done so in towns and villages away from Palermo itself, although the climatic scenes of *The Godfather Part III* were filmed outside the city's Teatro Massimo.

But if you are choosing to steer well away from contact with the mob during your stay in the city, just take sensible precautions and you will more than likely avoid having your valuables snatched by Vespa-borne delinquents, some of whom are destined to be sucked into the lower ranks of the big Mafia clans.

# History

Palermo is a city that has been ruled, settled and developed by several cultures. The first to discover it were the Phoenicians in the 7th century BC. They named it 'Ziz', meaning flower. Then came the Romans, who called it 'Panormus' (large port) because of the town's astonishing location on its own beautiful bay in the shadow of the limestone hulk of Monte Pellegrino. But, it was the Arabs who stamped the town with their art and culture when they conquered it in the 9th century, making it the Islamic centre of the Western world.

Under Arabic rule the town expanded beyond the old city centre of Cassaro (from the Arabic *Quasr* meaning castle or fort); on the harbour the castle or Kalsa (from *al Halisah* – the chosen one) flourished and was buttressed, becoming the primary residence of the Emir.

The Normans, led by Count Roger de Hauteville, arrived in 1072. In a non-violent transfer that mixed merchants, artisans, Muslims and other ethnic groups together, he allowed everyone to go about their daily lives as if nothing had changed. This mixture gave Palermo its beautiful Arab-Norman style of architecture.

Roger II, son of the Count and later crowned King of Sicily, spared no expense when it came to luxurious things. He built two extravagant palaces – La Zisa and La Cuba – and had formal Oriental gardens created for them. Roger indulged in succulent foods and wines and surrounded himself with intellectuals from around the world. This debauchery ended when Frederick II of Swabia (a region in southwestern Germany) took command of Sicily and Palermo in 1212, restoring the town's markets and harbour making it a business centre again.

The Swabians were ousted by the Angevins, who were conquered by the Spaniards, who were overthrown in turn in the

18th century by the Bourbons of Naples, who decorated Palermo with glorious baroque palaces.

The 19th century brought international trade and commerce, with Palermo outgrowing its boundaries. New streets such as the Viale delle Liberta, were built and lined with angular-style buildings; this was Palermo's last gasp at being an industrial centre. In the 20th century the bombings of World War II nearly destroyed the historical nucleus of the city, and then came a devastating earthquake in 1968. The medieval quarters went into decline as new, ugly buildings were built in the city's outer areas.

On centuries-old streets you will notice a sense of change and pride in the air. The city, thanks to its former mayor Leoluca Orlando and funds from the European Union, is in the midst of a city-wide re-evaluation and restoration programme to develop new uses for its magnificent historical areas and buildings.

*In evidence around Palermo is the triskele – the symbol of Sicily*

# Lifestyle

The Palermo of centuries ago was dignified, its buildings shone with colour and the air was free of pollution from cars, trains and buses. Nowadays the narrow streets are terribly clogged with traffic, pushcarts of foods and wares, and continuous construction making it is best to navigate Palermo on foot, or, to reach the outskirts or specific sights, by bus. Even cycling is dangerous, as Sicilians are fast

drivers notorious at stopping for nothing that gets in their way.

Palermo is run down, it is noisy, crowded, neglected, and, in some areas, seedy and still bombed out from World War II. This is a city with no place to go but up, one that has re-invented itself many times over and is on the verge of doing so again. There is a lot to see, even if some of the sights are in dire need of repair.

Twenty-first century Palermitans are showing great pride in their history and culture. Tourism is the main infrastructure and, to the delight of visitors, the city finally has the financial resources to dust off and preserve its beautiful theatres, cathedrals, palaces and museums.

As the capital of Sicily and its largest city, Palermo is a fast, brash and exciting place whose residents work hard and play hard. They have big city ways of dressing, dining, art, theatre, music and nightlife. That being said, Palermo boasts a large and visible gay/lesbian community of activists who contribute to the city scene artistically and culturally.

The current historical and cultural rejuvenation has brought along a new way of thinking: live in the moment but preserve the past. Most of Palermo, with its beautiful antique baroque, Byzantine, and Moorish architecture might seem like a place suspended in time. But walk one or two blocks in any direction and there is 21st-century architecture, restaurants, cinemas, nightlife and shops.

Like any other big city Palermo has its problems, but, this is a city not to be missed. Walk the streets and alleys, smell the aromas rising up from pushcarts and enjoy the traditional foods, attend cultural performances at theatres and museums, sit in the lush gardens and parks and absorb the sounds of this marvellous place.

*Streetmarkets are part of the Palermitan way of life*

# Culture

At one time Palermo was the first stop on anyone's Grand Tour. From a cultural standpoint it has been the preferred hangout of writers, artists and poets for centuries. They were drawn here by the erotic beauty and Arabic-influenced mysticism of the city and its surroundings.

Fortunately several nationalities left their indelible mark on Palermo's architecture and cultural scene. The city's museums have been working hard to preserve this history and to educate the masses with exhibits and seminars showing artefacts of the various cultures.

In that vein, the city has started a cultural initiative, 'Palermo Opens its Doors', which takes place every weekend in May. In the open doors event over a hundred monuments, that few people know about and are usually closed or abandoned, are 'adopted' by nearby schools and opened up to visitors. Thousands of children, studying their city's history and culture, act as tour guides for local people and tourists. They give the history and points of interest of churches, palaces, villas, works of art, squares and entire quarters of the city.

Another event, '100 Open Churches' (for information, ☎ 091.740.6035) is still in its infancy stages. This excellent initiative's aim is to open 100 abandoned churches and buildings where volunteer guides conduct tours. So far, they have opened 30, including the Palazzo Marchesi with its Scirocco rooms, the Chiesa di Santa Maria Valverde, which surrounds a neo-classical baroque interior, and the Convento di Santa Maria del Gesu.

So far both of these initiatives has been very successful and have

---

▶ *Teatro Politeama Garibaldi reflects the Palmeritan love of performance art*

helped to create awareness and develop rediscovery and re-appropriation of the city.

Palermitans are mad for live theatre, and, with the restoration of the once crumbling Teatro Massimo and Teatro Politeama Garibaldi, performances are in full swing with brilliant offerings of jazz, ballet, opera, concerts and classical music. For smaller venues featuring folk music and dance performances there is Teatrino Ditirammu del Canto Populare and Lo Spasimo: both are in the La Kalsa area. In summer months venues move to outdoor theatre at Teatro del Parco de Villa Castelnuovo showing operettas, musical comedy and ballet.

In summer an organisation called the Commune puts together open-air events, using local rock bands, which are either held in Giordano Inglese or green spaces throughout the city.

The websites Ⓦ www.palermotourism.com and Ⓦ www.bestofsicily.com feature extensive listings of galleries and theatres and give links to individual sights. Tourist offices stock the free bi-monthly magazine *Agenda,* which lists theatre productions, cultural events and museum times. It can also be found at some hotels.

It's a good idea to check posters placed around the city and in cafés, or the newspapers *Giornale di Sicilia* or *La Gazzetta del Sud*. For sporting events or scores, pick up a copy of either the *Corriere dello Sporto* or the pink newspaper *Gazzetta dello Sporto*. All of these are very popular and can be found at any news-stand.

---

▶ *Piazzas are dotted around the city enhancing views of major buildings such as the cathedral*

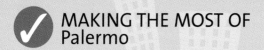

# MAKING THE MOST OF
## Palermo

# Shopping

Along the elegant Via Liberta are beautiful *haute couture* shops, including Dolce & Gabbana, Hermes, Luis Vuitton and Cartier. To get bargains on lesser known designer clothing and shoes try Via Roma.

Palermo is known for beautiful craft works; painted pottery, earthenware jugs and the handsomely decorated two-wheeled Sicilian horse carts. In existence throughout Sicily for more than eight centuries, tradesmen used the carts to carry their wares

through the streets of Palermo. During the height of their popularity in the 1920s there were as many as 5000 carts in Palermo alone. Sadly, the art of the cart creator is a dying one. There are only a few dedicated craftsmen who painstakingly hand-carve the carts and then decorate them with colourful panels denoting Sicily's centuries old battles between the cultural tribes. The best place to see antique carts or purchase new ones is at the Sicilian

*Bustling Vucciria market is typical of Palermo's street-shopping atmosphere*

Cart Museum behind the apse of Palermo Cathedral.

The sprawling market of the Vucciria quarter, between Via Roma and Via Vittorio Emanuele, gives one a good sense of the atmosphere of the city. In a small piazza surrounded by twisting, narrow streets lit by naked light bulbs even on a sunny day, the market holds the true aromas and sights of Palermo: fish stalls overflowing with swordfish heads; huge slabs of tuna hanging on hooks; fresh octopus sitting on blocks of ice; pyramids of blood oranges; rounds of cheeses; ropes of garlic; baskets of red and green peppers; and loaves of fresh baked bread.

Arrive early in the morning to watch the action as customers bargain and haggle with the fishmongers, farmers and bakers. Lunchtime is also a good time for a walk through as there are several good, inexpensive restaurants, some serving wine right out of the barrel, tucked into the alleys around the marketplace.

The Borgo Vecchio, between Piazza Sturzo and Piazza Ucciardone,

○ *Hand-painted porcelain and ceramics made ideal souvenirs*

is another noteworthy market. Along with the fish, meats, produce and pastries, are stalls full of colourful jewellery, porcelain, pasta bowls, clothing and leather goods. This is where the younger crowd gathers, as the market stays open late and is in the heart Palermo's night spots.

## USEFUL SHOPPING PHRASES

**What time do the shops open/close?**
A che ora aprono/chiudono i negozi?
*Ah keh awra ahprawnaw/kewdawnaw ee nehgotsee?*

**How much is this?**
Quant' è?
*Kwahnteh?*

**Can I try this on?**
Posso provarlo?
*Pawssaw prawvarrlaw?*

**My size is ...**
La mia taglia è ...
*Lah meeyah tahlyah eh ...*

**I'll take this one, thank you**
Prenderò questo, grazie
*Prehndehroh kwestaw, grahtsyeh*

**Can you show me the one in the window/this one?**
Può mostrarmi quello in vetrina/questo?
*Pooh oh mawstrahrmee kwehllaw een vehtreenah/kwehstaw?*

**This is too large/too small/too expensive**
Questo è troppo grande/troppo piccolo/troppo caro
*Kwestaw eh tropaw grahndeh/ tropaw peekawlaw/ trawpaw kahraw*

# Eating & drinking

Agriculture, fishing, cheese making and raising cattle have always played key roles in Sicily's economy. From the making of *cacivallo* (horse cheese) – so called because the rounds of cheeses are left to mature, two by two, linked by a piece of cord straddling a wooden beam – or *pecorino*, a cheese made from ewe's milk, to the renowned ricotta that is used in the preparation of the famed Sicilian crème horns and tutti-frutti, the production of cheese has been a rich traditional process.

In Palermo, as in other parts of Sicily and Italy, food is a way of life. The delicious aroma of Sicilian cooking fills not only the restaurants but streets and squares where kiosks and foodstalls prepare and serve *panelle*, fried chickpea pancakes and *crocchette*, croquette potatoes, to passers-by.

At most restaurants you can sample dishes that were invented in Palermo then spread across Sicily. One example is *pasta con le sarde*, a simple dish made with pasta, wild fennel, fresh sardines, anchovies, saffron, sultanas and pine nuts. It is served in both luxurious restaurants and simple family-style trattorias.

## ON A BUDGET

You can be budget conscious yet still eat well here. Street vendors and small cafés are abundant throughout the city.

Another way to cut costs is to shop the daily markets such as the Capo, behind the Teatro Massimo, where you can create a grand picnic sack of sausages, octopus, olives, salami, fresh fruit and loaves of crusty bread. Take your picnic to the steps of the teatro to dine and enjoy that universal pastime of people-watching.

## MENU CHOICES

In many restaurants the menus are gigantic, offering four courses;
*Primi* (first course, usually a pasta dish), *Secundi* (second course of a
fish or meat), followed by *Insalata* (green salad) or *Antipasti* (ham,
cheeses) and ending with *Dolci* (sweet).

It is not necessary to order all four, you can select two or even one
as long as they are from the two main courses. When it comes to
*dolci*, throw your diet to the wind and sample a traditional Sicilian
dessert, *cassata*, made with fresh ricotta, candied fruit and almonds.

## DRINKING

Palermitans enjoy their wine, particularly the sweet, heady wines
from Marsala. They like to drink it as an aperitif in the late
afternoon, or after dinner with cheese and fruit.

As in other parts of Italy coffee, or espresso, is served strong, dark
and thick enough to stand a spoon in, and is full of enough caffeine
to keep non-Italians awake for three days. True coffee aficionados
drink it unsweetened, and without *latte* (milk).

Coffee and wine may be an integral part of the scene in Palermo,
but, it is ice cream that Palermitans hold most holy in the food
chain. One of the city's glories are its *gelaterie* (ice cream shops).
While in Palermo get with the local custom and try a *brioche con*

---

**PRICE RATING**

The restaurant price guides used in the book indicate the
approximate cost of a three-course meal for one person,
excluding drinks, at the time of writing.

**€** = up to €15  **€€** = €15–30  **€€€** = €30–50  **€€€+** over €50

## USEFUL DINING PHRASES

**I would like a table for ... people**
Vorrei un tavolo per ... persone
*Vawrray oon tahvawlaw perr ... perrsawneh*

| | |
|---|---|
| **Waiter/waitress!** | **May I have the bill, please?** |
| Cameriere/cameriera! | Mi dà il conto, per favore? |
| *Cahmehryereh/cahmehryera!* | *Mee dah eel cawntaw, perr* |
| | *fahvawreh?* |

**I am a vegetarian. Does this contain meat?**
Sono vegetariano/vegetariana (fem.). Contiene carne?
*Sawnaw vejetahreeahnaw/vejetahreeahnah.*
*Contyehneh kahrneh?*

*gelato* (ice cream in a cinnamon bun) for breakfast, one bite and
you'll understand why Palermitans love it so.

## PRACTICAL DETAILS

Be prepared to dine very late, the restaurants that serve lunch do so
from 12.30–15.00, then close and don't re-open until 19.30 or later.
You will want to make your dinner reservation early in the day as
most restaurants are small and book up fast. Weekends are the
busiest time, when you need to make your reservations at least
three days in advance.

⏵ *It isn't hard to find a popular café or trattoria in which to lunch*

Cafés and *birrerias* are generally open late, restaurants close their kitchens by midnight. A good thing to remember is that many large restaurants are closed during August, and on Mondays and Tuesdays, several family-owned ones are even closed on Sundays, it is best to call ahead.

Credit cards are accepted in most of the city's large restaurants, as a rule; cafés and trattorias accept only cash. Tips are well received and there is no set amount, a 10 per cent tip is very generous, usually between €2 to €5 euros is acceptable. For bars, 30 cents is sufficient. Some upmarket restaurants add a service charge (it should be itemised on the bill) and if that is the case no further tip is necessary.

# Entertainment & nightlife

When the sun sets Palermo takes on a different look. The sounds of police sirens permeate the air; streets are empty of pedestrian traffic so it is best to keep to the main thoroughfares. In winter the city centre's bars and *birreiras* tend to close by midnight, but in summer the nightlife continues into the early morning hours.

### Bars & clubs

The area around Viale della Liberta has a lively street scene with cars cruising up and down blasting stereo systems. Bars and clubs come and go, so follow the crowds to the current favourite. Many of the new and trendy clubs are in the northern quarters of the city, particularly around Viale Regione Siciliana. These are upmarket, expensive places to see and be seen in, not really worth the bus or taxi ride to get there.

Via Principe di Belmonte with its flashy selection of bars and pastry cafés is a favourite of the young crowd. A haunt of students are the bars along the Via Candelai.

Another hot scene for nightlife is the trendy beach resort of Mondello 11 km (7 miles) from the city centre (see page 110), take bus no. 806 or 833 from either Piazza Sturzo or Viale della Liberta. The last bus returning to Palermo is at 23.00, while a taxi back to the city centre costs €30. Mondello's bars and clubs are the places to see and be seen. On summer nights the bars in the main square are overflowing, spilling out onto the Piazza Mondello, where local youths cruise the strip and open-air discos pulse with music.

Ice cream is a passion in Palermo, and one of the city's marvels is its *gelaterie* (ice cream parlours), many of which stay open late. All the better to serve the post-discothèque crowd their *brioche con gelato* (ice cream in a cinnamon bun), usually served as a breakfast pastry. Some of the best parlours are in the northern part of the city on Corso dei Mille, Via Villareale and at the lower end of Foro Italico.

## Cinemas & theatres

Hollywood and films have always held a fascination to Palermitans. One of their favourite pastimes is to frequent the many cinemas along Palermo's *cinema via* (movie road), the Via E. Amari. Here's a chance to learn Italian, all the movies are dubbed, no original language subtitles.

If you do speak Italian (or want to learn) look into some of the alternative smaller live performance theatres; the season runs from November to May.

**Teatro Siciliano** features productions in Sicilian dialect. ⓐ Zappala Via Autonomia Siciliana. ⓣ 091.543.380.

**Teatro Biondo** also has productions in Sicilian. ⓐ Via Teatro Biondo 11. ⓣ 091.582.364. ⓦ www.teatrobiondo.it

**Teatro Libero** specialises in avant-garde productions. ⓐ Salita Partanna 4, Piazza Marina. ⓣ 091.617.4040.
ⓦ www.teatroliberopalermo.it

## Listings

All of Palermo's tourist offices stock the bi-monthly magazine *Agenda*, which lists theatre times and productions.

The websites given below feature extensive listings on theatres, and cinemas and give links to individual sites:
ⓦ www.palermotourism.com
ⓦ www.bestofsicily.com or http://palermoit.ags.myareaguide.com

## Sport & relaxation

### SPECTATOR SPORTS

As in all other Italian cities football is big in Palermo and the team's pink and black colours much in evidence. Matches at La Favorita stadium draw huge and excitable crowds– for event dates, times or scores pick up a copy of the pink newspaper *Gazetta dello Sporto* or the *Corriere dello Sporto*.

### PARTICIPATION SPORTS

The best form of exercise while in Palermo is walking. That being said, if jogging or running is more to your liking you will not be alone at any of the city's open parks or green spaces: Parco d'Orleans by the University of Palermo, Giardino Inglese on Via Della Liberta or the largest park in the city, Parco della Favorita on Via Impertole Federico.

### Golf

With the generally mild climate you can play golf year round at locations near the city. Two courses that offer glorious views of mountains and the sea are located in Collesano (40 km/25 miles from Palermo), the Golf Club Collesano or the Le Madonie Golf Club. Both are situated between the Madonie natural park and the gulf of Cefalu. If driving take the A29 towards Cefalu; buses to Collessano leave from Stazione Centrale. Be sure to check at the station what number bus goes to Collesano as the buses change according to the season.

**Golf Club Collesano** ❶ 092.193.4387 or 091.698.0011.
**Le Madonie Golf Club** ❶ 092.193.4387. ❿ www.lemadoniegolf.com

## Tennis

Public tennis courts are located on Viale del Fante near the northern entrance of Parco della Favorita (bring your own racket). Circolo del Tennis TC2 has indoor hard surface and outdoor clay courts; rackets can be rented. It is best to call ahead to reserve a court.

**Circolo del Tennis TC2** ❷ Via San Lorenzo. ❶ 091.688.5360.
Ⓦ www.tcpa2.com/circolo.htm

## Cycling

If you really want to get your blood pumping and your heart racing ride a bicycle in Palermo traffic. You can get free bike rental (with a security deposit) at Via Principe Belmonte, the Giardino Inglese and Piazza Unita d'Italia.

**Kursaal Kalhesa** rents bicycles for around €6 per day ❷ Foro Italico 21. ❶ 091.616.2828.

**Toto Cannatella** (❷ Via Papireto 14a. ❶ 091.322.425) charges €10 per day.

## Watersports & extreme sports

Along with windsurfing, the Albaria Windsurfing Club (❷ Viale Regina Elena 89A. ❶ 091.453.595. Ⓦ www.albaria.com) offers boardsailing, catamarans and sailing on Mondello bay.

For more hair-raising excitement, contact Sky Brothers (❷ Via Spinuzza 51. ❶ 091.662.2229. Ⓦ www.extremeplanet.biz). Their web address, extreme planet, says it all; sky diving, parasailing, paragliding, mountain climbing and bungee jumping are just a few of their adventures.

A word of warning: check what is covered by your travel insurance before trying the more dare-devil activities.

# Accommodation

July and August, when locals head to the seaside resorts, are considered the low season in the city. With the exception of 10–15 July, when the festival honouring the city's patron St Rosalia takes place, hotel rooms are easy to come by at very good rates. It is still best to reserve as far in advance as possible to save having to search for a room late at night, and, to obtain the best room rate.

The main tourist office on Piazza Castelnuovo (☎ 091. 583. 847 ⓦ www.palermotourism.com) can assist with last-minute lodgings.

Hotel prices vary depending on the area of the city that you stay in. Those that are the most reasonably priced can be found on or near the southern ends of Via Maqueda and Via Roma between Stazione Centrale and Corso Vittorio Emanuele. In this area the general rule is the higher the floor the cheaper the price.

In the historical and cultural centres hotels will be more expensive. Most hotels, big or small, include a breakfast of some sort, either coffee and a pastry or a complete hot meal.

Fortunately for travellers, many of Palermo's hotels are located near public transportation, historical sights or cultural venues.

### HOTELS

**Hotel Cavour €** On the fifth floor of a charming old palazzo. Rooms are light and airy, centrally located for public transport. ⌂ Via A. Manzoni 11 (5th floor with a lift). ☎ 091.616.2759. ☎ 091.616.2759. ⓔ giopintos@libero.it

**Cortese €** There are several advantages to staying here; the terrific price, friendly staff and clean rooms, some overlooking the Ballaro

> **PRICE RATING**
> Hotels conform to a rating system, ranging from one-star hotels, where rooms may not have private facilities, to five-star luxury resorts. Breakfast is not usually included in the rates for budget and mid-range hotels. Prices for a single night in a double room for two persons are:
> **€** = up to €65  **€€** = €65–€100  **€€€** = €100–150
> **€€€+** = over €150

market. However, the dark side streets around the hotel can be a little daunting at night. ❸ Via Scarparelli 16. ❶ 091. 331. 722.

**Hotel Moderno €** A friendly, family-owned hotel offering small functional rooms. Nothing fancy, but the staff will make you feel very welcome. The 3rd and 4th floors have a lift. ❸ Via Roma 276 . ❶ 091.588.683. ❶ 091.588.260. ❶ Bus 101.

**Orientale €** This hotel has two connections to history, it was once part of the Royal Apartments, and, Mussolini stayed here. Rooms are basic but clean. ❸ Via Maqueda 26. ❶ 091.616.5727. ❶ www.albergooorientale.191.it ❶ Linea Rossa (red line) bus.

**Rosalia Conca d'Oro €** Charming rooms and a welcoming owner will make you feel like you are a treasured friend. It is close to Stazione Centrale so it can be noisy. ❸ Via Santa Rosalia 7, 3rd floor (no lift). ❶ 091.616.4543. ❶ 091.617.5852. ❶ Linea Gialla (yellow line) bus.

**Sicilia €** Good value, air-conditioning, private baths. Rooms around

the downstairs courtyard are the quietest. 🄰 Via Davisi 99.
🄣 091.646.8460. 🄦 www.hotelsiciliapalermo.it

**Hotel Elite €–€€** Recently refurbished, this eighteen room hotel is
in the heart of Palermo's theatre district. Its small colourful rooms
boast modern frescoes painted by a local artist. 🄰 Via Mariano
Stabile 136. 🄣 091.329.318. 🄕 091.588.614. 🄦 www.elitehotel.info

**Joli €–€€** The décor is a little on the dark and heavy side, but this
classy hotel is steps away from cultural venues. 🄰 Via Michele
Amari 11. 🄣 091.611.1766. 🄕 091.616.1765. 🄦 www.hoteljoli.com

**Sausele €–€€** Swiss-run hotel where rooms are small, clean and
airy and all have private bathrooms. Centrally located in the historic
section of the city. 🄰 Via E. Errante 12. 🄣 091.616.1308.
🄕 091.616.7525. 🄦 www.hotelsausele.it

**Ucciardhome Hotel €€** Located in the heart of the old city centre,
close to Villa della Liberta, this new boutique hotel's soundproofed
rooms are furnished in sleek, minimalist style. 🄰 Via Enrico Albanese
34/36. 🄣 091.348.426. 🄦 www.hotelucciardhome.com 🄝 Bus 101, 102.

**Posta €€–€€€** This ancient palace once belonged to a barones. Its
rooms are decorated with a splash of 1970s style. The prime location,
in the area of the archaeological museum, makes this a good choice
for women travelling on their own. 🄰 Via Gagni 77. 🄣 091.587.338.
🄕 091.587.347. 🄦 www.hotelpostapalermo.it

**Ai Cavalieri Hotel €€€** Situated near the Quattro Canti, this
boutique hotel offers 35 rooms, some with balconies, free internet,

breakfast, and is pet friendly. Garage parking is available at an extra charge. ⓐ Via Sant'Oliva 2. ⓣ 091.583.282. ⓕ 091.612.6589. ⓦ www.aicavalierihotel.it. ⓝ Linea Gialla (yellow line) bus.

**Massimo Plaza Hotel €€€** Located across from the Teatro Massimo, this elegant boutique hotel has been totally refurbished as part of the urban renewal of Palermo. Car park nearby. ⓐ Via Maqueda 437. ⓣ 091.325.657. ⓕ 091.325.711. ⓦ www.massimoplazahotel.com ⓝ Linea Rossa (red line) bus.

**Hotel Principe di Villafranca €€€** An elegant boutique hotel in an upper-class residential neighbourhood. Rooms are decorated with works by local artists; breakfast and parking are included within the rate. ⓐ Via G. Turrisi Colonna 4. ⓣ 091.611.8523. ⓕ 091.588.705. ⓔ info@principedivillafranca.it

**Centrale Palace Hotel €€€+** This venerable 19th-century mansion shows it age with style; crystal chandeliers, polished floors and excellent service. The superb top floor restaurant offers panoramic views of the city. ⓐ Corso Vittorio Emanuele 327. ⓣ 091.336.666. ⓕ 091.334.881. ⓦ www.centralepalacehotel.it. ⓝ Bus 104, 105, 139.

**Grand Hotel Villa Igiea €€€+** This 19th-century art nouveau masterpiece, 3 km (1.8 mile) north of the city in Aquasanta, was used as a summer resort by the Florio family, the first people to can tuna in Sicily. The interior was decorated by Italian art nouveau master Ernesto Basile. The hotel offers excellent service, elegant rooms with balconies, formal gardens and complimentary hourly shuttle service to and from the city centre. ⓐ Salita Belmonte 43. ⓣ 091.631.2111. ⓕ 091. 547. 654. ⓦ www.villagieapalermo.it

## YOUTH HOSTELS

**Baia del Corallo €** No frills, dormitory beds, shared bathrooms, but the main thing in its favour is its proximity to the beach. Located in Sferracavallo, 13 km (8 miles) and two buses from Palermo.
📍 Via Plauto 27. 📞 091.679.7807. 📧 ostellodipalermo@libero.it.
🚍 Bus 101 from Stazione Centrale to the stadium, transfer to bus 628 and get off at the Hotel Bellevue stop after Sferracavallo.

**Casa Marconi €€** On the expensive side and a bit of a bus trek to get there, but it's new, modern, sparkling clean and has only private rooms and bathrooms. 📍 Via Monfenera 140. 📞 091.657.0611.
📠 091.657.0310. 🌐 www.casamarconi.it 🚍 Bus 246 from Stazione Centrale to the hospital at the end of the line, cross onto Via G. Basile then turn left onto Via Monfenera.

## CAMPING

There are two campsites at Sferracavallo, a half-hour bus ride from Palermo; take bus 616 from Piazza Vittorio Veneto on the northern end of Viale della Liberta. In view of the distance involved, 13 km (8 miles), and the price of the hostels, unless you hanker for life under canvas it might be worth staying in a budget hotel in the city.

**Dell'Ulivi €** Very basic, cottages, bunk beds, coin-operated hot showers. 📍 Via Pegaso 25. 📞 091.533.021.

**Trinacria €** Across from the sea, small basic cottages that sleep two to four people. Hot showers (included in rate), pizzeria on the premises. 📍 Via Barcarello. 📞 091.530.590.

● *The terrace of a city centre hotel can be a great place to relax*

# THE BEST OF PALERMO

Whether you are on a flying visit to Palermo or have a little more time to explore the city and its surroundings, there are some sights, places and experiences that you should not miss. For the best attractions for children, see pages 150–151.

**TOP 10 ATTRACTIONS**

- **Palazzo dei Normanni** Site of an Emir's palace but now home to the Sicilian parliament (see page 73).

- **Cappella Palatina** Mosaic scenes of Christ in the magnificently decorated 12th-century chapel (see page 74).

- **Royal Apartments** A room fit for King Roger is finally open for public viewing (see page 73).

- **Cattedrale** A huge Norman relic, with many later additions, that is impossible to miss in more ways that one (see page 67).

🔻 *A visit to the cathedral is a must on your city itinerary*

- **La Martorana and San Cataldo** Red golf-ball domes and another medieval church (see pages 62 and 65).

- **Gallerie Regionale Sicilia** Fabulous works of art in one of the country's best galleries, which specialises in medieval art (see page 102).

- **Museo Archeologico Regionale** A temple to Palermo's history from the Phoenician to the Roman eras. A highlight are the carvings from the temples of Selinunte (see page 88).

- **Orto Botanico & Villa Giulia** Stop and smell the flowers at two oases near the city centre. The botanic garden displays some exotic specimens (see pages 82 and 84).

- **Museo delle Marionette** Lots of puppets, marionettes and even Punch and Judy in a museum that will fascinate both adults and children (see page 102).

- **La Zisa** See how the nobles lived and view the collection of Islamic art in the recently restored palace (see page 89).

Your brief guide to seeing the best that Palermo has to offer, depending on how much time you have.

## HALF-DAY: PALERMO IN A HURRY

To get a sense of Palermo's history spend a few hours walking the narrow streets of the original town, the Quattro Canti, around the Palazzo dei Normanni. Built by the Arabs in the 9th century as the Emir's palace, it was abandoned by them in 938, rescued by the Normans and later by the Spanish in the 17th century.

Continue exploring with a walk through the tiny streets of the Albergheria district. Bordered by the Via Maqueda and Corso Vittorio Emanuele, this is a lively area day or night with cheap places to dine and drink.

If your visit to Palermo is in the evening, stroll the wide boulevards that surround illuminated monuments and cathedrals after dinner. Or take in a performance at the Teatro Massimo, one of the regional theatres, or head to the cinema.

## 1 DAY: TIME TO SEE A LITTLE MORE

Follow on the heels of the half-day itinerary above with tours of the some of the city's beautiful churches.

The Cappella Palatina was the private chapel of Roger II (see page 74), housed inside the Royal Apartments the walls are entirely covered with magnificent 12th-century mosaics. The Cattedrale offers more Norman architecture and tombs of the Swabian and Norman royal families.

Also in that area are the churches of San Cataldo with its red golf-ball shaped domes and La Martarana considered by many to be the finest surviving building in the medieval city.

## 2–3 DAYS: SHORT CITY BREAK

A longer stay factors in more time to explore areas outside the city centre. In La Kalsa, the Arabic quarter near the sea, the aroma of spices and Arabic specialities emanating from the many cafés is sure to whet your appetite. A visual feast is the 15th-century Palazzo Abatellis and the Galleria Regionale di Sicilia. Take a bus to the Museo Internazionale delle Marionette or the Museo Archeologico Regional. The superb castle, La Zisa, offers a wonderful collection of Islamic art.

When it is time to take a break from art, history and castles, or you feel the need for some green space, walk, or sit in the delightful Parco della Favorita, admire the formal gardens and the Chinese style pavilion Palazzina Cinese, and people watch.

## LONGER: ENJOYING PALERMO TO THE FULL

This offers the opportunity of discovering the area. You might consider short bus, train or ferry trips outside of Palermo. Sunbathe for a day in Mondello (see page 110),
explore the duomo in Monreale, on the city's outskirts (see page 114), or head west an hour or so to the seaside towns of Trapani and Marsala (see page 124). Kick back and rest for a day or two on the tiny island of Ustica 60 km (37 miles) north-west of Palermo. For a nature break hike through the Monte Pellegrino Nature Reserve and be rewarded with amazing views at the top.

🔽 *Escape to Mondello if time permits*

## Something for nothing

You don't have to spend a lot on admission fees to see or learn about Palermo's culture. There are piazzas, parks and avenues, lined with monuments, churches, fountains, murals, gorgeous architecture and colourful gardens that can be enjoyed for free.

In public parks watch or join in a football game, be entertained

● *Murals provide a colourful and free spectacle in the Albergheria quarter*

by street artists, sit on the steps of a centuries-old church, overlooking a piazza, and participate in the best free show: people-watching. From June to September, city parks and open squares are venues for free theatre performances of musicals, ballet and folklore events.

All of Palermo's churches are free, offering a great opportunity to enjoy their liturgical art and magnificent interiors. An inexpensive bus ride will get you to the base of Monte Pellegrino where you can visit the chapel dedicated to Santa Rosalia, the patron saint of Palermo, and enjoy expansive views of the city below.

Wine bars are all the rage here, putting out a free smorgasbord of food to tempt young professionals. So, get out the evening clothes and join them, as for the price of a drink, you can dine well. During daylight walks or sightseeing treks through the city, be on the look out for cafés and bars that offer this, then return in the evening.

Festivals bring lots of free goods; concerts, parades, live theatre and fireworks displays to name a few. The summer is fraught with festivals, the largest one, *Festino di Santa Rosalia*, lasts for six days, 10–15 July. During this time the city literally shuts down to celebrate the life of Santa Rosalia who saved Palermo from the plague in 1600. It is invaded by travelling theatrical and musical shows all offering plays about the life of Santa Rosalia. The culmination comes with a monumental procession and fireworks display. February brings the baroque Carnivale, celebrating Palermo's history with citywide masked balls and parades.

Food is a staple at any of the city's festivals; the streets and piazzas are clogged with kiosks of regional specialities, where you can sample for nothing or eat inexpensively.

# When it rains

A rainy day presents a good opportunity to explore some of Palermo's smaller, less crowded, out-of-the-way museums. Or to escape inclement weather and for a taste of something a little different – not to say slightly macabre – go underground into the catacombs or join a tour of the canals.

### Oratorio del Rosario di San Domenico

Located in the old section of the city behind the church of San Domenico, this jewel of a chapel is adorned with some the best baroque sculpture in Palermo. Built in the 16th century by the Knights of Malta, it was decorated by the master of stucco sculpture, Giacomo Serpotta, who devoted his life to creating oratories like this.

🅐 Via di Bambini 16. 🛈 091.332.779. 🕒 Mon–Fri 09.00–13.00, 14.00–17.30, Sat 09.00–13.00. Free admission. 🚍 Bus 107 or Linea Rossa (red line) bus.

### The Museo della Fondazi Mormino

Housed in the beautiful Banco di Sicilia building is a brilliant collection of paintings and artefacts. On exhibit are colourful Italian majolica dating back to the 16th century, an impressive collection of Greek vases, maps, rare coins, 19th-century paintings of seascapes by Antonino Leto and beautiful portraits of European women by Ettore de Maria Bergler.

🅐 Viale della Liberta 52. 🛈 091.625.519. 🕒 Mon–Fri 09.00–13.00, 15.00–17.00. Admission charge. 🚍 Bus 101, 102, 702, 704.

### Catacombe dei Cappuccini

The crypts of the Capuchin convent, built in 1651, contain thousands of fully dressed mummified corpses of Capuchin friars, wealthy Palermitans, including women, and children that were buried there until 1881 when the custom was abolished. The site is both macabre and beautiful, with corpses on walls and in niches, many looking as if they are conversing with each other. A particularly beautiful and sad one is the corpse of a little girl, so perfectly embalmed even her hair ribbon is still intact.

The tomb of G. Tomasi di Lampedusa, author of the famous Sicilian novel, *The Leopard*, is in the adjoining graveyard.

ⓐ Via Cappuccini. ☎ 091.212.117, 🕒 Daily 09.00–12.00, 15.00–17.00. Admission charge. 🚍 Bus 327.

### Palermo Sottosopra (*ga'nat*)

Not to be missed, the *ga'nat* or water conduits, are canals that absorb moisture from the water table then run it for miles underground. First built in Persia in the 7th century, they were implemented in Europe after the fall of the Roman Empire. Palermo's *ga'nats* date from the Norman period. They were built by the *muganni,* or water masters, whose trade was handed down from father to son.

Tours of the water conduits meet at various places in the city, and if you would to join one then further information is available from the tourist office or from Cooperativea Solidarieta. It is best to contact them a couple of days in advance.

Cooperativa Solidarieta. ☎ 091.580.433. 🕒 Admission charge. Guided two-hour tours.

# On arrival

## TIME DIFFERENCES

Italy follows Central European Time (CET). During Daylight Saving Time (end Mar–end Oct), the clocks are put ahead 1 hour. In the summer, at 12.00 noon in Palermo, time at home is as follows:

**Australia** Eastern Standard Time 20.00, Central Standard Time 19.30, Western Standard Time 18.00
**New Zealand** 22.00
**South Africa** 12.00
**UK and Republic of Ireland** 11.00
**USA and Canada** Newfoundland Time 07.30, Atlantic Canada Time 07.00, Eastern Time 06.00, Central Time 05.00, Mountain Time 04.00, Pacific Time 03.00, Alaska 02.00.

## ARRIVING

### By air

Palermo's airport, **Falcone-Borsellino** (🕿 091.702.0111.
🌐 www.gesap.it) is 30 km (19 miles) north of Palermo and is served by many international and domestic airlines. Inside the terminal there are cash machines, money exchange bureaux (🕒 Mon–Fri, 09.00–16.00), car hire, and an English-speaking tourist office (🕒 Mon–Fri 08.00–24.00, Sat and Sun 08.00–20.00) where you can pick up free city and public transport maps which can also be purchased at newspaper stands around the city.

Airport taxis 🕿 091.591.662. They wait at the kerbside by the arrivals terminal. It is a 40-min trip into the city, costing around €50.

Airport buses 🕿 091.580.457. The Prestia & Comande link bus located outside the arrivals terminal stops at Via Lazio, Piazza

Ruggero Settimo in front of the Politeama Hotel, ending at Stazione Centrale. The buses run every 30-minutes from 06.30 until the last arrival flight of the day, the trip takes 60 mins and costs €4.65. Prestia e Comande ⓐ Largo Siviglia 5 ❶ 091.586.351 ⓦ www.prestia-comande.it.

## By rail

The train from mainland Italy, Italian State Railways, or Ferrovie dello Santo, crosses the Straits of Messina. The train drives straight onto the ferry – the cost of which is included in the train ticket. If you are travelling from within Sicily there is limited train service to Palermo from Messina (3 hrs), Caltinissetta (2 hrs) and Catania (3 hrs). All arrive at Stazione Centrale.

For information and tickets contact:

**Italian State Railways** – Ferrovie dello Stato ⓐ Piazza della Croce Rossa 1, Rome. ❶ 020.7724.0011. ⓦ www.fs-on-line.com or ⓦ www.ferroviedellostato.it

**Eurostar** ❶ 087.0518.6186. ⓦ www.eurostar.co.uk

**Rail Europe** ❶ 087.0584.8848. ⓦ www.raileurope.co.uk

**Travel Cuts** ❶ 020.7255.1944. ⓦ www.travelcuts.co.uk.

## By bus

A daily bus service from Rome departs Stazione Tiburtina at 09.00, arriving at Palermo's Via Balsamo bus station 12 hours later. Cost is approximately €35.50 one way, or €60.50 for the round trip.

**Segesta Internazionale Bus** ❶ 091.300.556 (weekdays), 091.320.757 (Sat–Sun and public holidays).

Several other bus companies offer service from other major cities in Sicily to and from Palermo.

**SAIS** ⓐ Via Balsamo 16. ❶ 091.616.6028.

**Cuffaro** ⓐ Via Balsamo 13. ☎ 091.616.1510.
**Segesta** ⓐ Via Balsamo 26. ☎ 091.616.7919.

### By sea

One of the prettiest and most leisurely ways of arriving in Palermo
is by sea. Ferries leave from various mainland cities.

Genova–Palermo operated by Grandi Navi Veloci; one ferry daily, a
20-hr journey.

Livorno–Palermo operated by Grandi Navi Veloci; three times a week,
a 17-hr trip.

Naples–Palermo by Tirrenia Line; one car ferry daily, an 11-hr journey.

Naples–Palermo operated by SNAV; one catamaran daily mid-April
to early Oct, a 4-hr journey.

Agents for Italian Ferry Services are:

**Grandi Navi Veloci** In the UK: c/o Viamare ☎ 0207 431 4560.
Ⓦ www.viamare.com. In Italy: ⓐ Via Fieschi 17, Genova. ☎ 010.55.091.
Ⓦ www.gnv.it.

**SNAV** In UK: c/o Viamare ☎ 0207 431 4560. Ⓦ www.viamare.com.
In Italy, Stazione Marittima, Napoli. ☎ 081.428.5111. Ⓦ www.snav.it
ⓔ mergelli@tin.it

**Tirrenia Line** In the UK c/o SMS Travel. ☎ 0207 373 6548.
Ⓦ www.tirrenia.it. In Italy, ⓐ Molo Angioino, Napoli.
☎ 199.123.199 from Italy, or 081.317.2999 from outside Italy.
Ⓦ www.gruppotirrenia.it

### DRIVING IN PALERMO

Avoid driving in Palermo as the traffic is horrendous and the streets
are narrow and crowded. And if that isn't enough, another problem
is parking. In the city proper there are only four municipal car parks.
Be warned, a city car park might have special arrangements with

nearby hotels, giving hotel guests priority parking. Large car parks are found on the outskirts of Palermo, which could mean a long walk or bus ride into the city centre. The cost for most car parks is approximately €30 for 24 hours.

If you must drive, the major thoroughfares are the A19, A20 and the A29. As you approach Palermo these join a loop road, the Viale Regionale Siciliana, and from this several marked exits can be taken into the city.

## FINDING YOUR FEET
Your first full day in Palermo try to factor in some early morning down time, find a centrally located park or café where you can relax

### IF YOU GET LOST, TRY ...

**Excuse me, do you speak English?**
Mi scusi, parla inglese?
*Mee scoozee, parrla eenglehzeh?*

**Excuse me, is this the right way to the old town/the city centre/the tourist office/ the station/the bus station?**
Mi scusi, è questa la strada per città vecchia/al centro città/l'ufficio informazioni turistiche/alla stazione ferroviaria/ alla stazione degli autobus?
*Mee scoozee, eh kwehstah lah strahda perr lah cheetta vehkyah/ahl chentraw cheetteh/looffeechaw eenforrmahtsyawnee tooreesteekeh/ahlla stahtsyawneh ferrawvyarya/ahlla stahtsyawneh delee ahootawboos?*

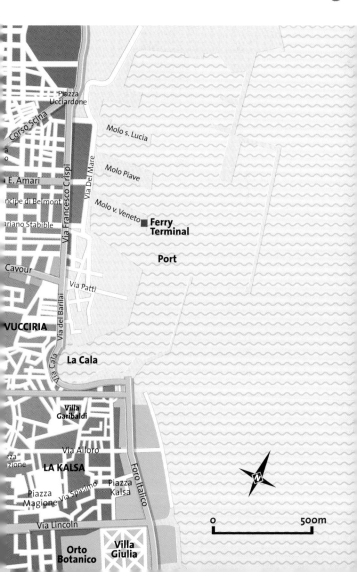

Piazza
Ucciardone

Corso Scina

Molo s. Lucia

Via Del Mare

Molo Piave

E. Amari

ncipe di Belmont

Molo v. Veneto

**Ferry
Terminal**

ariano Stabile

Via Francesco Crispi

**Port**

Cavour

Via Patti

Via del Barilai

**VUCCIRIA**

Via Cala

**La Cala**

**Villa
Garibaldi**

Via Alloro

zza
zione

**LA KALSA**

Foro Italico

Piazza
Magione

Via Spazimo

Piazza
Kalsa

Via Lincoln

**Orto
Botanico**

**Villa
Giulia**

0          500m

and acquaint yourself with the city. By doing this, you will have a chance to notice how beautiful, spacious and elegant Palermo is. To make the most of your visit, study your city and transport maps.

Treat Palermo as you would any other metropolitan city. Be conscious of your surroundings at all times; do not carry or show large sums of money, cameras or jewellery. After dark keep away from areas around the train or bus stations, late at night take taxis or walk only in well lit, heavily populated areas. Palermo has its share of motor scooters, and be warned – a few of their drivers are experts at snatching dangling purses, cameras or necklaces from pedestrians. In other words, try not to look like a tourist, keep all valuables close to you and out of sight.

## ORIENTATION

The medieval street system is alive and well in Palermo, making it easy for visitors to get lost. Note your starting location by remembering a major landmark or through street, and always carry a city map. The maps in this book show the main sights and streets, but some of the places listed are on smaller streets, so if you a planning a longer stay in the city it is worth acquiring a detailed map from a local bookshop or news-stand.

Begin your sightseeing in the Quattro Canti, the crossroads of Palermo's major streets; Via Maqueda, Via Vittorio Emanuele and Via Roma. The Quattro is bordered by Corso de Ruggeiro to the north and Foro Italico near the harbour to the south. This is the city's most heavily concentrated area of historic churches, palaces, and museums, many of which are within walking distance from each other.

Surrounding the Quattro Canti are the Ballaro and Vucciria market areas, good places to pick up a meal to go. If you get turned around you can ask for directions in any of the areas numerous shops or restaurants, or use the Via Maqueda as your guide, it crosses Palermo, becoming the Via Della Liberta in the modern section of the city.

## GETTING AROUND

Although walking is advocated in Palermo, you may tire and want to use public transport at some point. AMAT city buses (☎ 091.690.2690) cover Palermo as well as Monreale, Mondello and beyond. You can purchase a flat-fare ticket, €1.35 valid on any bus for two hours, or, an all-day ticket for €3.35. AMAT kiosks are at Stazion Centrale, Piazza Ruggero Settimo and Piazza Verdi, or anywhere you see the sign 'Vendita Biglietti AMAT'. All you need to do is validate one in the machine on the bus as you start your journey, for all-day tickets do it only on the first ride.

Two minibus services loop the city and popular tourist sights; Linea Gialla (Yellow Line; daily from 07.30–19.30) and Linea Rossa (Red Line; daily from 07.30–20.20). Tickets are available at AMAT ticket kiosks, €1 for two hours, or €3.30 for the day. City buses run from 04.00–23.00 daily. Bus ranks are outside the train station, Piazza Castelnuovo, at various points along Corso Vittorio Emanuele, and Viale della Liberta.

### Taxis

**Audioradio Taxi** ☎ 091.513.311 or 091.513.198.
**Radio taxi Trinacria** ☎ 091.682.5441 or 091.225.455.
    Taxi ranks are found at:
**Lido di Mondello** ☎ 091.513.311.
**Civic Hospital** ☎ 091.486.981.
**Massimo**, Piazza G. Verdi. ☎ 091.320.184.
**Piazza Indipendenza** ☎ 091.422.703.

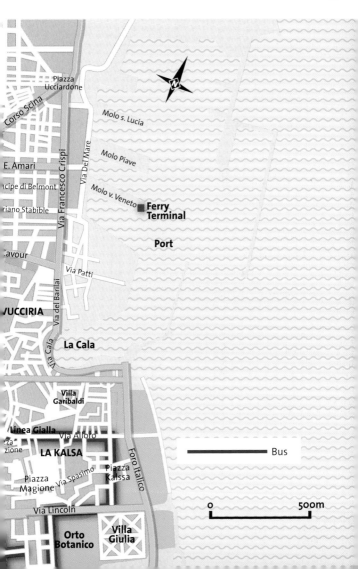

Piazza
Ucciardone

Corso Scina

Molo s. Lucia

Via Del Mare

Via Francesco Crispi

Molo Piave

E. Amari

cipe di Belmont

Molo v. Veneto

■ **Ferry
Terminal**

riano Stabile

**Port**

avour

Via Patti

Via del Barilai

**VUCCIRIA**

Via Cala

**La Cala**

**Villa
Garibaldi**

**Linea Gialla**

za

Via Alloro

zione

**LA KALSA**

Piazza
Kalssa

Foro Italico

Piazza
Magione

Via Spasimo

Via Lincoln

**Orto
Botanico**

**Villa
Giulia**

—————————— Bus

0                    500m

**Politeama** ☎ 091.588.133.
**Stazione Central FS** ☎ 091.616.2001.
**Stazione Notarbartolo FS** ☎ 091.343.506.
**Via Eman** Notabartolo. ☎ 091.625.1672.
**Via Malta** ☎ 091.616.2000 or 091.231.000.

## CAR HIRE

A piece of paramount advice – do not drive in Palermo city itself. That being said, the best way to explore the countryside is by car. When making your airline reservation enquire if an air/car package is offered.

There are six car hire agencies at the airport that also have offices in the city. To check rates or reserve go to ⓦ www.carhire.co.uk/car-hire/palermo-airport.html or ⓦ www.hispacar.com

Once you have your documents take time to familiarise yourself with the vehicle. Anyone who is accustomed to driving on the left will have a problem adjusting to roundabouts, traffic, two-lane highways, so stay alert and go slow.

**Avis** ⊟ Airport ☎ 091.591.684. ⊟ Via E. Amari 91. ☎ 091.586.940.
**Europcar** ⊟ Airport ☎ 091.591.688. ⊟ Via Cavour 77a ☎ 091.301.825.
**Hertz** ⊟ Airport ☎ 091.213.112. ⊟ Via Messina 7e. ☎ 091.323.439.
**Holiday Car Rental** ⊟ Airport ☎ 091.591.687. ⊟ Via E. Amari 85a. ☎ 091.325.155.
**Maggiore Car Rental** ⊟ Airport ☎ 091.591.681. ⊟ Stazione Notobartolo. ☎ 091.681.0081.
**Sicily by Car** ⊟ Airport ☎ 091.591.250. ⊟ Via M. Stabile 6a. ☎ 091.581.045.

▶ *The horseshoe-shaped old harbour is one characterful part of the city*

# THE CITY OF
# Palermo

# Quattro Canti & the Albergheria

A spacious octagon marks the intersection of the city's two main streets, Via Vittorio Emanuele and Via Maqueda. Built in 1611, Piazza Vigliena, or, as it is better known, the Quattro Canti, is not really a piazza but more a set of baroque crossroads that divide the city into quadrants. A short walk in any direction brings you to some of Palermo's most elegant piazzas, buildings and four magnificent churches: San Giuseppe dei Teatini, Santa Caterina, San Cataldo and La Martorana.

Also in the quattro is the University, making the area a haven for students and good, cheap cafés and bars.

The Albergheria district, bounded by the Via Maqueda and Via Vittorio Emanuele, has its own ambience, having been little changed for several hundred years.

## SIGHTS & ATTRACTIONS

### San Giuseppe dei Teatini
Don't let the simple façade of this magnificent 17th-century church fool you. The church was designed by Giacomo Besio in 1612, its interior, laid out in a Latin cross form, is a treasure trove of details; everything from a stunning encrusted ceiling, white and gold decorations and frescos, to 22 enormous stucco columns supporting the great dome, mostly restored from bomb damage in 1943.
❷ Via Vittorio Emanuele. ◔ Mon–Sat 07.30–12.00, 17.30–20.00, Sun 08.30–12.30, 18.00–20.00.

### Piazza Pretoria
Cross Via Maqueda to reach this lovely piazza centred with a

Via Malaspina

Via Giacomo Cusmano

Via Della Libertà

Via G. Dalla

Via Dante

Via Villa Florio

Via Goethe

Piazza Castelnuovo

Piazza S. Oliva

Piazza S.Francesco Di Paola

Via Ruggero Settimo

Corso C.Finocchiaro Aprile

Via Costantino Lascaris

Via Volturno

Piazza Verdi

Via Cavour

Teatro Massimo

Via D'Ossuna

Capo

Via Sant'Agostino

Via Del Candelai

Via Colonna Rotta

Corso Alberto Amedeo

Via Maqueda

Palazzo Archives-coville

Cattedrale

Porta Nuova

Via Vittorio Emanuele

Quattro Canti

Piazza Indipend-enza

Palazzo del Normanni/Capella Palatina

San Giuseppi

Piazza Pretoria

Corso re Ruggero

Via Porta di Castro

Gesu San Cataldo

San Giovanni degli Eremiti

Chiesa del Gesu

ALBERGHERIA

Via Roma

Via Albergheria

Piazza Rivoluz-ione

Via Maqueda

Via Garibaldi

Corso Tukory

Piazza G.Cesare

500m

Stazione Centrale

magnificent fountain, its 16 statues are divided by four sets of stairs leading to the largest fountain in the centre. The fountain was sculpted in 1555 by Francesco Camilliani and originally stood in the Tuscan villa of the Viceroy Don Pedro de Toledo. The Viceroy's son sold the fountain to the city of Palermo in 1574. It was shipped here piece by piece and installed in front of the Municipio (City Hall).

## Santa Caterina Church

Flanking the piazza is the church of Santa Caterina, a fine example of Sicilian baroque architecture, the inside of which is verdant with colour; deep reds and brilliant yellows filling crevices behind sculpted cherubs, Madonnas, lions and eagles. There's a marble panel (on the right as you enter one of the smaller chapels) depicting Jonah about to be swallowed by a ferocious whale.
🅐 Piazza Bellini

## Church of Santa Maria Dell'Ammiraglio (La Martorana Church)

The church's official name is Saint Mary's of the Admiral. It was built in 1143 by King Roger II's admiral, George of Antioch. Throughout the centuries the church has undergone many alterations. Peter of Aragon was crowned king here, and under the Spanish the church was given to a convent that was founded by Eloisa Martorana, it is from her that it derives its name: La Martorana.

Unfortunately, in the 17th century most of La Martorana's original Arab-Norman construction was scaled off and replaced with baroque. What does exist from that period are the church's spectacular mosaics: *King Roger being crowned by Christ*, *The Nativity* and *The Passing Away of the Virgin*. These are just three of

▶ *Quattro Canti is the impressive heart of the city*

## FRUTTA MARTORANA

*Frutta Martorana*, also known as *paste reale* and one of the most typical kinds of Sicilian *pasticcerie*, is named after the church that bears the same name. According to tradition, the origins of this delicacy can be traced back to medieval times when every convent specialised in making a different kind of confectionary. The ones made by the Benedictine convent of La Martorana in early November for the feast day of All Saints, were of marzipan, shaped and coloured to resemble different kinds of fruits. The tradition continues today; during the *Fiera dei Morti* at the beginning of November the district between Via Spicuzza and Piazza Olivella is invaded by brightly coloured stalls selling *frutta martorana* dolls and children's toys made from sugar.

Marzipan is also of medieval origin; the term is derived from the Arabic mauthaban which originally denoted a coin, then a unit of measurement and finally the container used to store the paste which is made with almonds, sugar and egg whites.

the many that decorate the interior spaces and the mosaics are attributed to master Byzantine craftsmen brought to Sicily from Constantinople by King Roger II.

The remaining exterior Norman elements are the bell tower, the domed roof and the external walls with blind arcading around the windows.

📍 Piazza Bellini 2, adjacent to Piazza Pretoria. ☎ 091.616.1692.
🕐 Mon–Sat 09.30–13.00, 15.30–18.30, Sun 08.30–13.00. Free admission. 🚌 Bus 101, 102.

## San Cataldo

Although not on as grand a scale as La Martorana, this dignified little 12th-century chapel, with its red golf-ball shaped domes, holds its own with its simplistic beauty. The church was never decorated save for the crenellations around the roof. In the 18th century it was Palermo's post office. Surrounding it is a pretty mosaic walkway, a pinch of colour in the otherwise bare Piazza Bellini.

ⓐ Piazza Bellini 2, adjacent to La Martorana. ❶ 091.616.1692.
🕐 Tues–Fri 09.30–17.00, Sat–Sun 09.00–13.00. Admission charge.
Ⓝ Bus 101, 102.

## The Albergheria

Within this district Via Maqueda is lined with beautiful palazzos, such as the 18th-century Palazzo Santa Croce behind which is a neighbourhood of narrow streets, cafés, markets and churches. Most of this was bombed in 1943 and has never been repaired, which only serves to add to the uniqueness of the area.

## Chiesa del Gesu Professa, Il Gesu (Church of Jesus)

The Jesuits arrived in Sicily in the mid-16th century and with the backing of the Spanish government they founded their first church here. The interior's baroque inlaid marble and relief work took over 100 years to complete. The church was heavily damaged in the bombings of 1943 and has only been partially rebuilt.

ⓐ Via Ponticello. ❶ 091.581.880. 🕐 Mon–Sat 09.00–13.00, 15.00–18.30. Free admission. Ⓝ Bus 101, 102, 103, 104, 107.

## San Giovanni degli Eremiti (Church of Saint John of the Hermits)

Situated in a lovely and peaceful garden near the Palazzo dei Normanni, is the deconsecrated church of San Giovanni degli

Eremiti. Built in 1132 on the site of an earlier mosque, its red roof with five squat domes are clearly the works of Moorish craftsmen. The church was a favourite of its founder, King Roger II, who granted

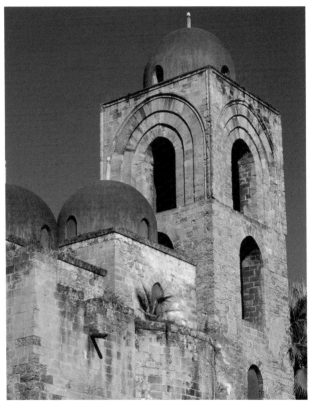

⬤ *The exterior of San Cataldo is bare save for those distinctive red domes*

the monks of San Giovanni 21 barrels of tuna a year, a special gift, considering that food products were controlled by the Crown at that time. The lacklustre interior has only a few broken frescoes. All that is left of the adjacent monastery are the 13th-century cloisters, whose twin columns surround a small garden.

🚇 Via dei Benedettini. 📞 091.651.5019. 🕐 Mon–Sat 09.00–13.00, 15.00–19.00, Sun 09.00–13.00. Admission charged. 🚌 Bus 109 or 318.

## The Cattedrale

Palermo's official cathedral is an impressive hulk of a building, more Norman than the Royal Palace. It was founded in 1185 by the English archbishop Gualtiero Offamiglio (Walter of the Mill) and was to be his base of operations in the city, but he didn't get the chance to use it as the Cattedrale was not finished until centuries after his death.

The Catalan Gothic south porch was added in the 15th century. Among its Gothic decorations are symbols of the four evangelists: Saints Matthew, Mark, Luke and John on the outer wall. Other works of striking ornamentation are the beautiful hand-carved wooden doors and the apses which retain original Norman details.

The neo-Classical dome was added in the 18th century when the church was totally refurbished. Of interest in the bland interior is the tombs containing the remains of some of Sicily's Swabian and Norman monarchs: Frederick II and his wife Constance, Henry VI and, at the rear, Roger II and his daughter Costanza d'Altavilla. In the small chapel to the right of the choir alter are the remains of St Rosalia, the patron saint of Palermo.

The treasury, or *tesoro*, has an impressive collection of rings, necklaces and the Imperial Gold Crown, which is set with precious stones, pearls and enamels. There's also a carved ivory staff made in Sicily in the 17th century and jewels belonging to Queen Costanza of

Aragon. Of particular note is a classical Roman sarcophagus decorated with the figures of the nine Muses and Apollo.

🅰 Via Vittorio Emanuele. ☎ 091.334.376.

🅦 www.cattedrale.palermo.it 🕐 Mon–Sat 07.00–19.00, Sun 08.00–13.30. Admission charged.

Treasury and crypt: access from the south transept of the church.

🕐 Mon–Sat 10.00–12.30, 14.00–16.00. Admission charged.

**Palazzo Archivescovile and the Porta Nuova**

At the western end of the Cattedrale is the Palazzo Archivescovile, at one time the archbishop's palace. The palazzo is entered through a 15th-century gateway and inside is the Museo Diocesano, which brings together various art work from the cathedral and churches destroyed in World War II. The museum is staffed by volunteers,

◆ *Palermo's cathedral was begun in the 12th century, but has later additions*

making the hours erratic – if closed you should still be able to take a look around in the courtyard.

As you exit the palazzo turn left up Via Bonello, where there is a lively antiques market, Mercato delle Pulci in Piazza Peranni.

### Via Vittorio Emanuele

If you return to the main street, you will note on the northern side of the Royal Palace the commanding Porta Nuova. Built in 1535, it memorialises Charles V's Tunisian exploits with carvings of Arabic figures.

### Il Capo

The apses of the Cattedrale border the Capo quarter, one of the oldest areas of Palermo. The only bit of green space in this congested, run-down area is the tiny, graceful Piazza del Monte, which is planted with trees and ringed by neighbourhood bars. There really is not much to see here save for a few decaying palaces, but, after looking at grand buildings, strolling here gives you a peek at a typical Palermo neighbourhood.

One alley, Via Porta Carini, is packed on either side with market stalls giving it the look of an Arab souk. Climb past decrepit buildings and closed churches, up to the Porta Carini, one of the city's medieval gates.

The market extends west to the edge of the Capo district and east along Via Sant'Agostino where you will find the church of Sant'Agostino built in the 13th century by the Chiaramonte and Sclafani families, scions of Sicilian aristocracy. The interior is decorated with some fine stuccoes by Giacomo Serpotta. On the Via

● *The Palace of the Normans is home to Sicily's parliament*

Sant'Agostino side of the building, behind the market stalls, is a deteriorating 15th-century doorway attributed to Domenico Gagini, one of a dynasty of skilled medieval sculptures who decorated many buildings in Sicily with their artwork.

## CULTURE

Palermo's churches, with their architecture, art and detailed decorations, are cultural havens. A visit to anyone of them is total immersion for the senses. The city also offers unique culture in its museums and palazzos.

### Palazzo dei Normanni (Palace of the Normans)

A royal palace has occupied this high ground since the 9th century when the Arabs built a fortress for the Emir. In 938 they abandoned it, transferring the Emir's residence, for security reasons, to the Kalsa. Then came the Norman's who enlarged it, turning the fortress into a palazzo and filling the interior with magnificent medieval European courts. In the 17th century the Spanish added the palazzo's long porch. Today, little remains of the original Arab-Norman structure. There is limited public access to the building as it now houses the Sicilian parliament.

ⓐ Piazza Indipendenza. ☎ 091.705.7003. ⏰ Mon, Fri, Sat 09.00–12.00. Other days by prior arrangement. 🚌 Bus 104, 105, 108, 109, 110, 118, 304, 309.

### The Royal Apartments

It is now only possible to make a guided visit to the Sala di Ruggero,

◀ *Mosaics – some dating back to the 12th century – decorate Capella Palatina*

Roger's Room. One of the original parts of the palazzo, it is covered with fantastic 12th-century mosaics depicting hunting scenes. As the apartments constitute a brief visit, it is best to do this first before descending one floor to the wonderful Cappella.

🚏 Piazza del Parlamento. ☎ 091.705.7003. 🕐 Mon, Fri, Sat 09.00–12.00. Other days by prior arrangement. 🚌 Bus 104, 105, 108, 109, 110, 118, 304, 309.

### Cappella Palatina

The chapel is considered by many to be the crown jewel of central Palermo. Built between 1132 and 1143 as the private chapel of Roger II, its magnificent interior, the cupola, three apses and nave are completely covered in outstanding mosaics. The oldest, completed in 1150 by Byzantine artists, are in the cupola and apses. Those in the nave, depicting the Old and New Testaments, were completed 20 years later by local craftsmen. The colours are so vivid they seem to leap out at you. Scenes depict Christ blessing, open book in hand, and Christ enthroned between Peter (to whom the chapel is dedicated) and Paul.

The Arab history of Palermo comes out in the chapel's Arabic ceiling with its carved wooden stalactites, patterned marble floor and, by the pulpit, an extraordinary, intricately carved Norman candlestick measuring 4 m (13 ft) in height.

🚏 Piazza del Parlamento. ☎ 091.705.7003. 🕐 Mon–Fri, 09.00-12.00, 15.00–17.00, Sat 09.00–11.45. Free admission. 🚌 Bus 104 ,105, 108, 109, 110, 118, 304, 309.

### Teatro Massimo

Built in 1875 by Giovanni Battista Basile, whose neo-classical design is said to have been influenced by Charles Garnier's contemporary plans for the Paris Opera, it was finished by Basile's son Ernesto who added the two distinctive Liberty-style kiosks in front of the theatre. The one on the right, built of wood and wrought iron, is the Vicari al Massimo Kiosk, while the one on the left, made of iron, is the Ribaudo Kiosk.

The interior is richly gilded with pink marble, and colours of rich reds, blues and golds grace the walls of the theatre and the Sala Pompeiana where the nobility once gathered before a performance. In the auditorium is a massive domed ceiling carved into the shape of a flower.

For many years the opera house was the centre of high society in Palermo, with a grand selection of musical performers to its credit. Sadly it was allowed fall into disrepair and, in 1974, it was closed for restoration. As is the way in Sicily this project became bogged down in political and financial problems, and the theatre did not reopen until 1997, some 23 years after its closure. You don't have to attend a performance to appreciate its beauty; guided tours in English are conducted throughout the year, except during rehearsals.

ⓐ Piazza Giuseppe Verde. ⓣ 091.605.3515.

ⓦ www.teatromassimo.it ⓔ Guided tours in English Tue–Sun 10.00–16.00 every 30 mins. Admission charged. ⓝ Bus 101, 102, 103, 104, 107, 122, 125.

## RETAIL THERAPY

Palermo has its share of shops, everything from *haute couture* to 'gently used' fashions from designer labels. There are many shops specialising in ceramics, art, wine, needlepoint, embroidered fabrics and linens. Some visitors come to Palermo just to purchase ceramics.

Many shops are closed on Monday mornings, the general shopping hours are Mon–Fri 09.00–13.00, 15.30–19.00, Sat 09.00–13.00, 16.00–20.00.

**DeSimone** This family-owned business has been creating majolica-style stoneware since 1920. They also create beautiful tiles with scenes of the Sicilian countryside, seascapes and landscapes. When you are there, inquire about visits to their factory in Palermo where the stoneware is made.
🅐 Via Gaetano Daiti 13B. ☎ 091.584.876. Ⓝ Bus 103, 106, 108, 122.

**Le Gi di Valentino** If you're looking for a funky outfit, perhaps something that exudes Marilyn Monroe, then you have hit the jackpot with this place. The style here is wenchy, tarty and elegant.
🅐 Via Ruggiero Settimo 99-101. ☎ 091.324.197.
Ⓝ Bus 101, 102, 103, 124.

**Frette** Frette's high thread-count sheets and ultra soft linens are reportedly used at the Vatican. Not only does that mean that they are famous, it also means high prices, but worth it. The shop is a delight of fabrics; nightgowns, tablecloths, towels and tapestries to name a few. 🅐 Via Ruggiero Settimo 12. ☎ 091.585.166.
Ⓝ Bus 101, 102, 103, 124.

**Libreria Altro Quandro** Along with the usual bestsellers (mostly in Italian) you will find a good amount of revolutionary, socialist, gay-liberated and politically correct books here. Being Sicily, gay books are upstairs tucked away in the back of the shop.
🅐 Via Vittorio Emanuele 125. ☎ 091.611.4732. Ⓝ Bus 103, 104, 105, 108, 110, 139, 224, 225, 389, 824.

## TAKING A BREAK

After feeding your senses on culture and shopping comes the time to re-fuel the body in the middle of the day. The old section of Palermo offers a host of cafés, pizzerias (more pizza is eaten in Palermo than in any other part of Italy), and ice cream palaces. From neighbourhood hangouts, to elegant and upmarket, you are bound to find several to suit your tastes.

**San Francesco €** Owned by the same family that owns Antica Focacceria San Francesco (see page 93), this is a good old town ice cream palace with tables in the square.
🄰 Piazza San Francesco. ☎ 091.320.064. 🕐 until 04.00.
🚍 Bus 103, 105, 225.

**Santoro €** Near the Palazzo dei Normanni on the edge of a wooded piazza. A shady respite on a hot day of sightseeing.
🄰 Piazza Indipendenza. 🚍 Bus 104, 105, 108, 109, 110, 118, 304, 309.

**Bellini €–€€** Housed at the back of the Teatro Bellini, the large pizza ovens are operating all day. At night sit at outdoor tables underneath La Martorana church – one of the city's most romantic locations. Arrive before 20.30 to avoid the crowds. 🄰 Piazza Bellini.
🕐 Closed Wed and Dec–Jan. 🚍 Bus 101, 102.

**Tratorria Normanni €–€€** A favourite with locals. Their speciality dish is *spaghetti al Normanni*, a wonderful mix of shrimps, aubergines, fresh vegetables and grated peanuts. Best to arrive early to snag an outside table. 🄰 Piazza della Vittoria 25 (off Piazza Indipendenza).
🕐 Closed Sun. 🚍 Bus 104, 105, 108, 110, 118, 304, 309.

**Trattoria Mafone (da Massimo) €€** This neighbourhood trattoria is just a few blocks behind the cathedral, with tables out into the piazza. Lots of great seafood is served here. Try the house speciality, *fettucine da Massimo*, a colourful pesto dish with fresh clams and shrimps.  Piazza Papireto 15. Bus 101, 102, 103, 104, 107.

## AFTER DARK

The Quattro Canti and Albergheria areas are lovely to stroll in at night. Most of the palazzos and churches are illuminated, adding to the romance of the streets and avenues. Before dinner stop for an aperitif in one of the lively cafés.

**Il Garage €** A great little hole-in-the-wall restaurant whose affable Tunisian owner prepares delicious homemade fish, lamb and couscous dishes. It's difficult to find, just ask anyone in the neighbourhood for 'Mario' and they'll direct you. Piazza Ecce Uomo, across from Il Gesu. 333.490.6356. Bus 102, 103, 104 and 107.

**Casa del Brodo €–€€** In business for over a century, this place attracts locals and students to its two small dining rooms. Order the house speciality, *carni bolliti* (boiled meats), as you will not be disappointed with this delicious assortment of herb-encrusted meats. Good value for the money. Reservations recommended. Corso Vittorio Emanuele 175. 091.321.655. Wed–Mon 12.30–15.00, 19.30–23.00. Bus 103, 104, 105, 118 or 225.

**Al Santa Caterina €€** Housed in a 16th-century palazzo, this intimate restaurant offers good Sicilian fare. Dine under the stars on a

balcony overlooking the corso. ⊖ Corso Vittorio Emanuele 256–258.
🕒 Closed Wed. Ⓝ Bus 101, 102.

**Caffe d'Oriente (Caffe Arabo) €€** A Tunisian menu of rich spicy rice
and couscous dishes is offered here along with outstanding salads,
marzipan sweets for dessert and belly-dancers! Reservations
recommended. ⊖ Piazza Cancelliere 8 (up Via Monte Vergine from
Corso Vittorio Emanuele). ☎ 091.326.832. 🕒 Tues–Sun 12.30–15.00
and 19.00–23.00. Ⓝ Bus 101, 102.

🔺 Eating places in Palermo remain lively and busy well into the evening

# Via Roma & the Vucciria

Starting at the Stazione Centrale and ending at Piazza Sturzo (below Piazza Ruggero Steeimo), Via Roma is a 20th-century addition to Palermo. Connected to Via Maqueda by several narrow alleys this area is not particularly beautiful or interesting, consisting of tall granite apartment blocks with hotels. The one break in this granite and cement jungle is Via Divisi to the east, a narrow street full of bicycle shops.

The surrounding area's retail commodities are grouped according to their trade; ironmongery, children's clothes and ceramics all have their own individual spots. After this, Via Roma is all clothes and shoe shops, with a few cafés and restaurants.

## SIGHTS & ATTRACTIONS

### Gardens and Green Space
When you want to escape the traffic, crowds and noise of the city allow the time to have a sit down, or take a stroll through some of Palermo's wonderful parks and gardens.

### Piazza Marina
The Arabs were a people who appreciated the joy of a green oasis. It was their culture who introduced gardens to Palermo. The Normans expanded on this with their parklands and summer palaces. In the heart of Palermo, at Piazza Marina, lies the Giardino (Garden) Garibaldi, the walks of which are lined with banyan trees, their gigantic exposed roots spreading out across the grounds under towering palms. In the 10th century this was where jousting contests were held and executions performed. Nowadays

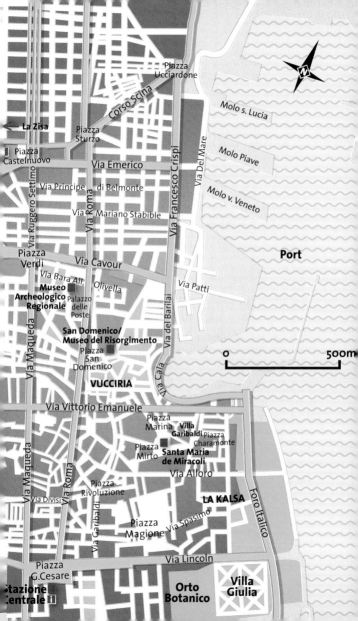

Piazza
Ucciardone

Corso Scina

Molo s. Lucia

La Zisa

Piazza
Sturzo

Piazza
Castelnuovo

Via Emerico

Via Principe di Belmonte

Via Mariano Stabible

Molo Piave

Molo v. Veneto

Via Del Mare

Via Francesco Crispi

Port

Piazza
Verdi

Via Cavour

Via Ruggero Settimo

Via Roma

Via Bara All, Olivella

Museo
Archeologico
Regionale

Palazzo
delle
Poste

Via Patti

Via del Barilai

San Domenico/
Museo del Risorgimento

Piazza
San
Domenico

Via Maqueda

VUCCIRIA

Via Cala

0                    500m

Via Vittorio Emanuele

Piazza
Marina

Villa
Garibaldi

Piazza
Charamonte

Piazza
Mirto

Santa Maria
de Miracoli

Via Alloro

Via Maqueda

Via Roma

Piazza
Rivoluzione

LA KALSA

Via Divisi

Via Garibaldi

Piazza
Magione

Via Spasimo

Foro Italico

Piazza
G.Cesare

Via Lincoln

Stazione
Centrale

Orto
Botanico

Villa
Giulia

pensioners gather here to pass the time playing cards and gossiping. This peaceful spot is surrounded by palaces, cafés and restaurants.

The largest palace on the square is the 14th-century Palazzo Chiaramonte on the east side of the piazza. The most interesting portion of the palazzo is the façade with its two tiers of windows surrounded by magnificent stone inlays. From 1685 to 1782 the palazzo was the home of the Inquisition before it became the city's law courts. Today it is the administration building for the university and is only open to the public for special exhibitions.

On the southwest corner is the 16th-century church of Santa Maria dei Miracoli, built in the Renaissance design.

West of the piazza is Via Merlo and at no. 2 is the **Palazzo Mirto** (🕒 Mon–Sat 09.00–19.00, Sun 09.00–13.00; admission charged). Built in the late 18th century, it is one of the few palazzos in Palermo that still has its original furnishings. The first floor is the only portion open to the public, worth going in for the magnificent ceilings, the Chinese Room, the baldacchino and the tapestries, which are all still in excellent condition. 🚍 Bus 101, 102, 103, 104, 107.

## Orto Botanico

This beautiful space is a favourite with Palermitans. The gardens and water lily pond were laid out in 1795. The most impressive specimen is the 150-year-old banyan tree with its gigantic roots sprawling over the ground. Growing here are species of plants from all over the world. Among the curiosities are the South American *Bombacaceae* and *Chorisias* plants identifiable by their swollen,

⏵ *Exotic specimen plants entice visitors into the Orto Botanico*

prickly trunks. In the spring they are covered with brilliant pink flowers which turn into fruit. ✉ Via Abramo Lincoln 2B. ☎ 091.623.8141. ⏰ Weekdays 09.00–20.00, Sat and Sun 09.00–13.00. Closed public holidays. Admission charged. Ⓝ Bus 139, 211, 221, 224, 226, 227.

## Villa Giulia

Next door to the Orto Botanico is another peaceful oasis, the Villa Giulia. Created in 1778 and enlarged in 1866, the park bears the name of its patron, Giulia Avalos Guevara, the wife of the ruling viceroy of the time. Covering the grounds are acres of aromatic

flowers, a children's train, bandstand, deer and ducks. ❷ Via Abramo Lincoln. ❶ 091.740.4028. ⏱ Daily 08.00–20.00. 🚌 Bus 139, 211, 221, 224, 226, 227.

## CULTURE

Once you cross Via Vittorio Emanuele you will come to the church of Sant'Antonio, the stairs on the side of the church lead down to the Vucciria quarter with its enormous marketplace, churches and museums.

❂ *The grounds of the Villa Giulia are a peaceful haven in a busy city*

### San Domenico

On the north side of the marketplace is San Domenico, an extraordinary 18th-century church. The baroque façade rises in three ordered tiers of Doric and Corinthian columns and square pilasters framing the statue of St Domenic. The enormous interior is separated into aisles and the nave, with a chapel off each bay and holds tombs of famous Sicilian painters, poets and writers. The church is an impressive sight at night when the entire front is lit.
🅐 Piazza San Domenico. 🅘 091.584.872. 🅛 Mon–Fri 09.00–11.30, Sat–Sun 17.00–19.00. Free admission. 🅝 Bus 101.

### Museo del Risorgimento

The buildings adjacent to the church belong to the Sicilian Historical Society (*Societa Siciliana per la Storia Patria*) with the small but interesting Museo del Risorgimento, which has an excellent collection of exhibits pertaining to the 19th-century Italian anti-Bourbon revolt, and containing mementoes of Garibaldi. Adjacent to the museum are some beautiful 14th-century cloisters.
🅐 Piazza San Domenico 1. 🅛 Mon, Wed, Fri 09.00–13.00; ring for entry. Closed Aug. Free admission. 🅝 Bus 101.
To visit the cloisters 🅘 091.329.588.

### Piazza delle Poste

Further up Via Roma the huge concrete chunky building on the left is Piazza delle Poste, built by the Fascists in 1933. Today it is Palermo's main post office. The only good thing about the building is the pink colour of the exterior walls, which softens the blow of looking at it and lends a nice hue at night when the building is lit. Around the corner from this hulk is the Piazza Olivella and the church of Sant'Ignazio Martire all'Olivella with its elegant baroque interior.

◯ *Palazzo Mirto offers a rare chance to examine the original interior decor*

Next to the church is the city's excellent archeological museum in
what were once the cloisters and buildings of a 16th-century convent.
❸ Piazza Olivella. Ⓥ Bus 101, 102, 103, 104 and 107.
Sant'Ignazio Martire all'Olivella ● Mon–Sat 09.00–10.00,
17.00–18.00, Sun 09.30–12.00.

## Museo Archeologico Regionale

Although it could use a good dusting and it is not state-of-the-art, this is one of the grandest archeological museums in Italy and well worth a visit.

The museum is stocked with artefacts dating from prehistoric times to the Roman era. Contained in several buildings, the oldest one from the 13th century, is an excellent collection of monumental Sicilian finds from Phoenician, Punic, Greek, Roman and Saracen periods.

Enter the ground floor through the smaller of two cloisters where you will find displays of anchors from the sea off the Sicilian coast. Another small room has Phoenician art, most notably a pair of sarcophagi dating to the 5th century BC. Beyond that is a room with Egyptian and Punic finds including the Pietra di Palermo, a black diorite slab known as the Rosetta Stone of Palermo (the other three parts of the Stone are in Cairo and London), dating back to 2700BC. Etched on the stone in hieroglyphics is 700 years of Egyptian history. There is also a Punic one recovered from the harbour in Marsala with the figure of a priest worshipping the god Tanit.

Further along the cloister is dedicated to Roman sculpture, on the left is Emperor Claudius enthroned in the style of Zeus. Other rooms showcase early Greek-carved stelae and several inscribed tablets. Beyond here the exhibits are mostly of Greek origin, the stone lions-head water spouts from the Victory Temple at Himera, 5th century BC.

The most important collection of the museum is the Sala di Selinunte, unique stone carvings (metopes) from Temples A-G at Selinunte on the southwest coast. The friezes were used to adorn the temples and show mythological scenes. The earliest friezes are from the 6th century BC, the panels depict the gods of Delphi, the Sphinx, the rape of Europa, and Hercules and the Bull. The most vivid panels, such as Perseus beheading Medusa (his head and torso pointing directly out at you), date back to the 5th century BC and were unearthed from Temples C and F.

Also on exhibit are panels from the early 5th century BC Temple E, they portray Hercules battling an Amazon, the marriage of Zeus and Hera, Actaeon being savaged by dogs, and Athena and the Titan.

Retrace your steps to the small cloister for the stairs up to the first floor where you will find many other exhibits of interest, among them lead water pipes retrieved from an archeological site at Termini Imerese (now Therma Himeraia) – originally settled by

## THE PALACE OF LA ZISA

West of the centre of Palermo is the palace of La Zisa. Taken from the Arabic al-aziz or 'magnificient' this towering palace was begun by William I in 1160 and finished in 1175 by his son, William II.

La Zisa was built in North African style, as a king's retreat. At one time it was stocked with beautifully laid out gardens and rare and exotic beasts. The palace languished for centuries within a large private estate and, today, is surrounded by blocks of modern apartments. But, the good news is that La Zisa has been mostly restored and displayed within it are wonderful Islamic mosaic designs, a large collection of Islamic art and artefacts. Unfortunately, the gardens are still a work in progress.

🅐 Piazza Gugliemo il Buono (near Piazza Camporeale at the end of Via Dante). 🕿 091.652.0269. 🕐 Mon – Sat 09.00—19.00. Admission charged. 🚌 Bus 124 from Piazza Politeama.

Greeks in the 7th century BC it is still famous for its healing waters, Also on display are more than 12,000 votive terracotta figures and some carved stone heads found at Solunto, a place that had been settled by the Phoenicians in the eighth century BC, and then later by the Greeks who surrendered it to the Romans during the First Punic War.

The second floor of the museum is not to be missed as it is here that there is a room full of splendidly preserved Roman mosaics. The largest, measuring 10 m (33 ft) in length, was excavated from Piazza della Vittoria in Palermo. The *Triumph of Neptune* mosaic dates from the 2nd century AD, while another from the 3rd century AD shows Orpheus with a lyre surrounded by friendly beasts.
🅐 Piazza Olivella 24. ☎ 091.611.6805. 🕐 Tues–Sat 08.30–18.00, Sun 09.00–13.00. 🚌 Bus 101, 102, 103, 104, 107.

## RETAIL THERAPY

If you want high-end fashion this is not the quarter for it, head over to Via della Liberta and Via Principe di Belmonte if you are after Dolce & Gabbana, Hermes, and Armani. What you will find in the Via Roma and Vucciria quarter is a marketplace full of stalls selling fish, vegetables and pastry along with housewares, shoes and clothing. The narrow streets surrounding the quarter have a few shops offering some unique goods.

**Postolato Liturgico** Devout Catholics from around the world flock to this museum-like shop. Staffed by white clad nuns from the order of the Paoline Pedice (Pious Disciples of the Divine Master), the shop

◀ *This district is renowned for its street markets*

specialises in church related finery. Glass cabinets hold gold chalices and medallions, many of them encrusted with gemstones, and stunning liturgical robes. 🅰 Corso Vittorio Emanuele 454.
🕐 091.651.2467. 🚍 Bus 103, 104, 105, 108, 110 or 118.

**Giuseppe Gramuglia** The name of the game here is fabric, hundred of bolts in every conceivable texture, design and colour. If your taste runs to the rope, fringe and tassel look then this is the place for you.
🅰 Via Roma 412–414 (corner of Via Principe di Belmonte).
🕐 091.583.262. 🚍 Bus 104, 107, 122, 124, 224 or 225.

**Barone Confezioni-Abbigliamento-Corredi** Catering to Palermitans for over six decades, this department store is your only chance for fashionable clothes in the quarter. 🅰 Via Abramo Lincoln 146.
🕐 091.616.5626. 🚍 Bus 139, 211, 221, 224, 226, 227, 231, 234, 250 or 971.

## TAKING A BREAK

**Caffe San Domenico €** Observe the action at the early morning Vuccerio marketplace while you munch on delicious pastries and sip strong Sicilian coffee at outdoor tables. 🅰 Piazza San Domenico.
🕐 early morning to late evening. 🚍 Bus 101, 103, 104, 107.

**Cana Wine Bar €** Located in a medieval building behind Piazza Marina, this charming intimate wine bar, open only in the evenings, is an ideal spot for an aperitif after a day of exploring. 🅰 Via Alloro 105. 🚍 Bus 101, 103, 104, 107.

**La Corrida €** Located in a row of bars across from the archeological museum. Good for a snack and a rest. 🅰 Piazza Olivella 9. 🕐 Open mid-afternoon to late evening. 🚌 Bus 101, 102, 103, 104, 107.

**Franco U Vastiddaru €** A simple place in a great location the pizzas, salads, and burgers are pricey but quite good. Eat in at the counter or take your order outdoors to the piazza. 📍 Piazza Marina 1. 🚌 Bus 101, 103, 104, 107.

**Ilardo €** Ice cream is a passion in Palermo, and the Ilardo – which has been in business for decades – is known for its excellent ice cream. 📍 Foro Italico 12 (at the end of Via Alloro towards the water). 🚌 Bus 101, 103, 104, 107.

**Renna's Self Serve €** Simple cafétéria style restaurant, good for an informal lunch or dinner or if you are in a hurry. Nothing fancy just delicious Italian food at reasonable prices. 📍 Off Via Roma near the Hotel delle Palme. 🚌 Bus 104, 107, 122, 124, 224, 225.

**Tabuca €** A cosy, quiet little spot great place to relax with a glass of wine and people watch. 📍 Piazza Marina 6. 🕐 Open early afternoon to late evening. 🚌 Bus 101, 102, 103, 104, 107.

## AFTER DARK

The Piazza Marina is ringed with restaurants and cafés as are many of the narrow streets and alleys surrounding it and the many churches in this area.

**Antica Focacceria San Francesco €** An old time pizzeria that must be doing something right because it has been open since 1834. Great inexpensive pizzas, focaccia sandwiches, *panelle* (deep-fried chickpea fritters) and *arancini di riso* (rice balls stuffed with tomatoes, peas and mozzarella). ❷ Via A. Paternostro 59 (off Corso Vittorio Emanuele and opposite the church of San Francesco). ❶ 091.320.264. ⏱ Daily 10.00–24.00. ❷ Bus 103, 105 or 225.

**Le Pergamene €** Alfresco restaurant adjacent to the Giardino Garibaldi with main courses that focus on pasta, smoked seafood, and grilled meats. The menu also boasts two dozen varieties of pizza. ❷ Piazza Marina 48–49. ❶ 091. 616.6142. ⏱ 17.00–24.00. ❷ Bus 103, 105, 225.

**La Traviata €** Tucked away in a quiet alley steps from the Museo Archeologico. The pasta choices are excellent and inexpensive. ❷ Piazza Olivella 18. ❷ Bus 101, 102, 103, 104, 107.

**Mi Manda Picone €€** The Sicilian wines served here are excellent, the food flavourful and the prices are affordable. The view will take your breath away, a few steps up from the restaurant's entrance is the façade of the Romanesque gem Chiesa di San Francesco. ❷ Via Alessandro Paternostro 59. ❶ 091.616.0660. ⏱ Mon–Sat 19.30–23.00. ❷ Bus 103, 108, 164.

**Il Mirto e la Rosa €€** Once a strict vegetarian restaurant (its menu is still heavy on the vegetables) the 'Myrtle and the Rose' now serves well prepared fish and meat dishes. The aromas of North African prepared vegetable couscous and spicy pasta dishes are heady in this well-run establishment. Reservations recommended. ❷ Via Principe di Granatelli 30. ❶ 091.324.353. ⏱ Closed 25–31 Aug. ❷ Bus 101, 102, 103.

**Tratorria Stella €€** Although the sign over the door reads 'Hotel Patria', the hotel is no longer there but the excellent restaurant is. Specialities consist of barbecued lamb and fish dishes. Dine under the stars in the elegant medieval courtyard. 🄰 Via Alloro 104 (corner of Via Aragona). 🄱 Closed Mon in winter, Sun evening July, Aug.

**La Fenice €€€** You won't satisfy your craving for pasta here, they don't serve it. This charming place located directly on the Piazza Marina specialises in grilled meats and fish and delightful rice dishes. Try the grilled sausage *alla pizzaiola*, traditional pork sausage grilled with tomatoes, onions, garlic and parsley. Service is excellent as is the wine list. Reservations recommended. 🄰 Piazza Marina 52-53. 🄲 091.616.2230. 🄱 Sept–July 12.30–15.30, 20.00–24.00, Aug daily 19.30–24.00. 🄽 Bus 103, 105, 225.

**La Cambusa €€€** This elegant quiet restaurant overlooking Piazza Marina specialises in fish dishes. There's also an excellent antipasti buffet. Menu prices do not include the restaurant's 10 per cent service charge. 🄰 Piazza Marina 16. 🄲 091.584.574. 🄴 leopoldo@lacambusa.it 🄽 Bus 103, 105, 225.

**Sant'Andrea €€€+** This stylish restaurant is the reason you brought that chic black dress or that suit and tie. Located near the Piazza San Domenico and the Vucceria market where most of the restaurants ingredients come from; they don't have menus, the delicious creations are at the whim of the chef. The fantastic desserts are made on the premises, and there's a superior wine list. Reserve well in advance for an outside table. 🄰 Piazza Sant'Andrea 4. 🄲 091.334.999. 🄱 Closed Tues and January. 🄽 Bus 101, 103, 104, 107.

## La Kalsa – the Historic Quarter

'Balarm, the immense city of beauty, the wondrous splendid sojourn, the world's vast metropolis, adorned in elegance... Balarm has buildings of such beauty that travellers come from afar to the well-known marvels of its architecture.' Al Idrisi (1099–1166).

The 'Balarm' that Muslim geographer Al Idrisi refers to in this quote is Palermo. It was written at the time when La Kalsa, from Arabic *khalisa* (meaning pure) was the city's cultural and intellectual centre. Al Idrisi was the court geographer to the Emir of Sicily which was under Arab rule before King Roger ascended the throne.

Al Idrisi's knowledge and competence caught the attention of Roger II, the Norman King, who invited him to produce an up-to-date world map. He constructed a circular map of pure silver that weighed 400 kilograms and precisely recorded on it the seven continents with trade routes, lakes and rivers, major cities, and plains and mountains. Al Idrisi described the world in *Al-Kitab al-Rujari* (Roger's Book), also entitled *Nuzhat al-Mushtag fi Ikhtirag al-Afag* (The Delight of Him Who Desires to Journey Through the Climates). He spent most of his life in service to King Roger II.

Designed and built by the Saracens, La Kalsa is one of Palermo's oldest quarters. It lies behind the port and was heavily bombed in 1943, when many people were killed and countless buildings destroyed. The ruins were thrown into the sea and, as a result, the Foro Italico, a short distance from the seafront, was created with the rubble.

Today, there is still more work to be done, but almost the entire district has undergone a complete restoration, new squares have been created, one of which is Piazza Magione, laid out like an English meadow, the palazzi and monuments have been dusted and

Via Emerico

Via Mariano Stabible

Via Francesco Crispi

Via Del Mare

Molo v. Veneto

**Port**

Via Cavour

Via Patti

Via del Barilai

Via Cala

**La Cala**

Via Vittorio Emanuele

**Museo delle Marionette**

Via Alessandro Paternostro

Via Butera

Via Alloro

Via Roma

**La Gancia**

**Galleria Regionale**

**Santa Teresa alla Kalsa**

Piazza Rivoluzione

Via Garibaldi

**KALSA**

Piazza Magione

Via Spasimo

Via Torremuzza

Piazza Kalsa

Foro Italico

Via Magione

**Santa Maria dello Spasimo**

**Porta Dei Greci**

Via Lincoln

Piazza Cesare

**Stazione Centrale**

**Villa Giulia**

0                    500m

cleaned and cultural centres such as the Chieso dello Spasimo and Teatro Garibaldi host numerous concerts year round of jazz and classical music, many of them free. From mid-June to mid-September the quarter is jumping with the KalsArt Festival (Ⓦ www.kalsart.it; see page 10), a cultural extravaganza of live music, theatre, and cinema events that take place throughout the La Kalsa district.

La Kalsa is bounded by the port of La Cala on one side and Via Garibaldi and Via Paternostro to the east and west, and by Via Vittorio Emanuele and Via Lincoln to the north and south. Via Butera and Via Alloro are two of the main thoroughfares that cross it. The

● *Palermo's tradition of puppetry dates back several centuries*

heart of the quarter is Piazza della Kalsa, containing many of the city's most interesting Arab-Norman architecture, monuments, museums, parks and churches.

### THE OLD HARBOUR – LA CALA

The thumb-shaped inlet of the old city harbour, La Cala, was once Palermo's main port. Its unfortunate decline started in the 16th century, when silting caused the water to recede to its current position. The fishermen and trade ships moved north-west to docks off what is now Stazione Marittima. Today La Cala's primary function is as marina to the yachts of the well-heeled. The docks are great for a stroll around, and to enjoy the excellent views over the little harbour to Monte Pellegrino in the distance.

## CULTURE

### Opera dei Puppi (Puppet Theatre)

Opera dei Puppi, or Puppet Theatre, embodies a strong sense of Palermo's culture, so much so that in 2001 it was declared a masterpiece of oral tradition by UNESCO.

The marionette tradition dates back to the 16th century. These masterpiece creations, many of which are hundreds of years old, are brightly painted and costumed puppets made of wood and controlled by a wire attached to the head and right hand of each puppet. A dying art across the rest of the island, Palermo's puppet theatre is still going strong and much beloved.

The puppet masters tell stories of bandits, romance, heroism,

duels and of course feature Punch and Judy in their traditional stage. This is not to be missed and great fun for all age groups.

Puppet Theatre tourist performances are held at the Museo delle Marionette (see page 102), ❷ Vicolo Niscemi 5. ❶ 091.328.060, or search out the inexpensive small theatres frequented by locals: Argento ❷ Via Pietro Novelli 1. ❶ 091.611.3680; near the Museo Archeologico at Cuticchio Mimmo ❷ Via Bara all'Olivella 52. ❶ 091.323.400; Teatro Ippogrifo, ❷ Vicolo Ragusi 6, off the Corso Vittorio Emanuele near the Quattro Canti. ❶ 091.329.194.

### Santa Teresa alla Kalsa

Start your rambling at the entrance to the quarter the Porta dei Greci, beyond this lies the Piazza della Kalsa and church of Santa Teresa alla Kalsa, a magnificent baroque church that took architect Paolo Amato 20 years (1686 to 1706) to complete. In the commanding facade are two orders of Corinthian columns, a monumental feat for the time in which the church was built. ❷ Piazza della Kalsa. ❶ 091.617.1658. ❸ Bus 103, 105, 139.

### Via Alloro

From the Piazza della Kalsa walk north on Via Torremuzza passing the beautiful stone-framed Noviziato dei Crociferi and, on the opposite side of the street, the Santa Maria della Pieta, designed by Giacomo Amata. Continue walking until you reach Via Alloro, La Kalsa's main street in the Middle Ages head west along Via Alloro for a close-up view of this decaying district that lost many beautiful palazzi and is still under repair from the 1943 bombings.

---

◀ *It isn't just children who enjoy a performance at the Puppet Theatre*

## Museo delle Marionette

On the harbour side of the quarter, near Foro Italico, you will find the Museo delle Marionette. The museum is devoted to puppets of all kinds, the Sicilian *pupi*, puppets based on characters from the French *chansons de geste*, marionettes, articulated puppets operated with strings, shadow puppets, and Punch and Judy in their traditional booth. ❸ Via Butera 1, near Piazzetta Niscemi. ❶ 091.328.060. ⓦ www.museomarionettepalermo.it ⓒ Mon–Fri 09.00–13.00, 16.00–19.00. Admission charged. ⓐ Bus 103, 105, 139, 225.

Walk further down Via Butera and you will come to the recently restored Palazzo Butera, with its 17th-century facade facing out over the Foro Italico. This elegant palazzo was home to the Branciforte family, at one time the wealthiest family in Sicily. Tours are by appointment only. ❶ 091.611.0162

This entire quarter was destroyed in the bombings of 1943. It has been rebuilt into an unattractive promenade, the Foro Italico, complete with an amusement park. The only good thing in it is the views it offers of Monte Pellegrino. Still, on nice evenings, this is a very lively place where locals stroll arm in arm enjoying ice cream from the several gelateria palaces that surround it.

## Galleria Regionale Sicilia (Regional Gallery)

Housed in the 15th-century Palazzo Abatellis, and designed by Matteo Carnelivari in 1490, is what is considered by Italian art aficionados as the greatest gallery of regional art in Sicily and one of the finest in Italy, the Galleria Regionale with its brilliant medieval art collection. The palazzo holds its own among all the brilliance of the inside art, it still retains elements of its Catalan-Gothic and Renaissance origin in its doorway and courtyard. Heavily damaged in the World War II bombings, its interior was restored in 1954 by

Carlo Scarpa, one of Italy's foremost contemporary interior designers. For each important work of art contained here, Scarpa used different materials and colours to display the art in the best possible way and enhance the natural daylight to the fullest.

The museum has 16 exhibition rooms, which alternatively display paintings and sculpture masterpieces by artists Francesco Laurana, Antonello da Messina, Antonello Gagni and his school, Domenico Gagni, Serpotta and others. Laurana's white marble bust of the Spanish infanta *Eleonora of Aragon*, a study in peace and tranquility, can be found on the ground floor in room 4. Room 5 is devoted to works by the noted Gagini's, an eye catcher is Antonello Gagini's *Archangel Michael*.

The back wall of room 2 has the magnificent 15th-century fresco the *Triumph of Death*. This chilling study casts a cruel and realistic figure of Death as an archer sitting astride a galloping, skeletal horse, trampling people who are in the full blush of youth, and whom he has slain with his arrows. It hauntingly depicts the facial expressions of the old and sick as they plead hopelessly for oblivion as Death ignores them and rides towards a group of wealthy citizens who are apparently unconcerned by his approach. Formerly attributed to a Catalan painter the fresco is now regarded as a Gothic work and is attributed to the school of Pisanello, Veronese Antonio Pisano, known as Pisanello as he was the son of a Pisan draper.

Of the excellent 15th-century Sicilian art on this floor the most notable work is by Antonello da Messina, the ethereal *Our Lady of the Annunciation*; painted in 1473 it is considered to be one of da Messina's finest works. The brightness of the colours, the blue of the mantle, the pale brown of the complexion, the yellow of the pulpit, is remarkable. The purity of the Virgin's oval face is enhanced by the mantle framing it.

The masterpiece *Malvagna Tryptich* by Dutch painter Ian Gossaert, known as Mabuse, covers an entire wall. The *Malvagna*, painted in 1510, depicts the Virgin enthroned with Child and angels. 🄰 Palazzo Abatellis, Via Alloro 4. ☏ 091.623.0011. 🕑 Fri–Mon 09.00–13.30, Tues–Thur 09.00–13.30, 14.30–19.30. Admission charged. 🚌 Bus 103, 105, 139 or the Linea Gialla (yellow line bus).

## La Gancia

The 15th-century church of La Gancia, or Santa Maria degli Angeli, next to the Galleria Regionale, has more works of art by the Gagini family in the way of sculpted fragments and reliefs. Built by the Franciscans in the late 1400s the church has undergone numerous alterations that have modified its appearance, most particularly on the interior. Remaining of the original exterior are the square profile and rustication.

The church's baroque interior with its 16th-century artwork is currently undergoing a massive restoration by Sicilian architect Giovanni Nuzzo. When completed it is worth a visit to view the magnificent late-1500s organ by Raffaele della Valle, the elegant marble pulpit and Antonello Gagini's relief tondoes of the Annunciation on either side of the altar. 🄰 Via Alloro 27 ☏ 091.616.5221. 🕑 Mon–Sat 09.30–12.00, 15.00–18.00, Sun 10.00–12.30. 🚌 Bus 103, 105, 139 or the Linea Gialla (yellow line).

## Santa Maria dello Spasimo

Built inside the walls of the Kalsa in 1506, this church and convent were the work of Giacomo Basilico. It was Basilico who commissioned Raphael to paint *Lo Spasimo di Sicilia*, which was installed here in 1520 but is now in the Prada Museum in Madrid.

Building the church was a painstakingly slow process, it was not completed when the threat of war with Turkey made it necessary to build a Spanish bastion behind the church. Afterwards the complex was transformed into a fortress, a theatre, in 1624 it became a hospice for plague victims, and finally a hospital for prostitutes. It was abandoned in 1986. The church and hospital have been restored and now are venues for cultural events such as the Scuola Europea di Music Jazz.

Accessible to the public is the area around the 16th-century cloisters, endowed with simple, elegant lines. Beyond these is the church, an excellent example of Catalan-Gothic style. The interior consists of three naves, with a tall slender nave reaching up toward the roofless top and the open sky, and ending with a gorgeous multilateral apse.

The original entrance walls contain two side chapels. The one on the left, with the rounded dome, gives access to the bastion, which is now a lovely garden. ⓐ Via dello Spasimo. Ⓝ Bus 103, 105, 139.

**Piazza della Rivoluzione**

It was from here, in 1848, that the anti-Bourbon uprising began. In the centre of this pretty little piazza is an elaborate fountain depicting a king feeding a serpent.

From this piazza Via Garibaldi leads south, marking the end of the route that Garibaldi took in May 1860 when he entered the city marching north up Corso dei Mille and into what is now Via Garibaldi. Palazzo Aiutamicristo, one of the largest 15th-century palaces designed by Matteo Carnelivari, is at ⓐ Via Garibaldi 23. Ⓝ Bus 103, 105, 139.

**Piazza Magione and its surroundings**

Walk around the south side of the palace to the church of La

Magione standing at the end of a palm-shaded lane of Piazza Magione. This excellent example of Arab-Norman architecture was built in 1151 for the Cistercians. In 1197 Henry IV gave it to the Order of the Teutonic knights for use as their headquarters. It remained in the knights hands for over 300 years.

The church was heavily damaged during World War II, but the cloisters were spared and their treasures are phenomenal. There is a Judaic tombstone re-carved into a marble holy water receptacle. In the room between the cloister and chapel is a fresco of the crucifixion and opposite it is a rare plaster interpretation of the fresco, the only existing example of a fresco model in Sicily. It shows the great detail and planning that went into the work. Alongside this is a small Arab-Norman column carved with a Koranic inscription in Kufic Arabic, a first millennium angular script used for inscribing on hard surfaces and extant throughout much early Islamic art.

The walls are lined with before and after photographs showing the façade of the church before it was restored to its original Arab-Norman design in the early 1900s. ⓐ Via Magione. ⓛ Daily 09.30–19.00. ⓝ Bus 103, 105, 139.

Returning to Piazza Magione you will find an idyllic park that is a popular spot with Palermo's young set. It is a good spot to sit and relax.

## RETAIL THERAPY

La Kalsa district's narrow streets are full of tiny shops that specialise in jewellery, liqueurs, silver, books and embroidery. The high fashion shops, as mentioned before, are in the area around Via Della Liberta. And, of course there are the street markets. The closest ones to La Kalsa are the Vucciria at Piazza San Domenico and the Ballaro in the Albergheria district at Piazza Casa Professa.

**Di Bella** Located near the Capo marketplace, Di Bella is one the most distinctive jewellery stores in Palermo. Featured along with stylish rings, bracelets and necklaces are top brand watches.
🅐 Via Carini 22. ☎ 091.320.818. 🚌 Bus 104, 107.

**Tutone** Since 1813 the Tutone family has been providing Palermitans and visitors with a traditional drink that dates back to the Arabs, Anise Unico, water flavored with aniseed. Along with this refreshing pick-me-up the shop also carries lovely decanters of liqueurs and aperitifs. 🅐 Via Garibaldi 41. ☎ 091.616.1280. 🌐 www.tutone.it. 🚌 Bus 103, 105, 139.

## TAKING A BREAK

Around Piazza della Kalsa indulge yourself with a delicious treat called *babbaluci* – baby snails. The aroma of the snails marinating in a mixture of olive oil, chopped parsley, garlic and red pepper permeates the air. Vendors sell them in paper cones called cornets. Take a noontime break under a tree or on a bench and enjoy.
🅐 Piazza della Kalsa. 🚌 Bus 103, 105, 139.

**Parco Litterario Giuseppe Tomasi di Lampedusa €** This cultural centre and wine bar dedicated to the Sicilian author has an excellent wine list, and also offers antipasti, panini and good granita. There is a lovely cobbled terrace perfect for relaxing with a glass of Sicilian wine. 🅐 Vicolo della Neve all'Alloro. 🌐 www.parcotomasi.it

**Kursaal Kalhesa €–€€** A great place to meet young locals, most of whom are fluent in English. With its prime location in a restored palace near Piazza Marina, this is where Palermo meets New York

SoHo. Read English-language newspapers, listen to live entertainment, go online at the internet café, or pick up tourist information at the travel agency.

The upstairs restaurant serves Sicilian and Tunisian house specialities of artichoke pasta with a radicchio cream sauce, lemon flavoured swordfish with shrimp, and a local delicacy, lentils grown on the island of Ustica and flavoured with squid ink.

Fort Umberto 1. 091.616.7630. Tues–Sun 11.30–14.00, 16.00–24.00. Bus 101, 102, 130, 104, 107.

## AFTER DARK

La Kalsa is just as dangerous as it is fascinating. Keep your wits about you at all times. It's relatively safe during the day, but at night the labyrinthine streets are dark and it is best to take a taxi.

**Villa Niscemi €** Rustic bar usually overflowing with a crowd of 25–45-year-olds. Good value for the money. Piazza Niscemi 55. 091.688.0820. Daily 19.00–27.00. Closed Mon in July, Aug. Bus 614, 615, 645, 837.

**Al Covo de'i Beati Paoli €€** Great location, right on Piazza Garibaldi, outdoor tables, busy on weekends. Great pizzas. Piazza Marina 50. Closed Mon in winter.

**Genio Trattoria €€** Small family-run trattoria offering good seafood and grilled meats. Piazza San Carlo 9 (Piazza Rivoluzione). Bus 103, 105, 139.

*Head out of the city to historic towns and villages, such as Monreale*

# Mondello

When the summer sun burns hot, when old men on the square seek a place in the shade, when children tire of seeing churches and monuments, head for the beach. For Palermo residents and visitors alike that means Mondello Lido. At one time Mondello was a snobbish retreat for the Sicilian upper crust, evoking the most fashionable parts of the French Riviera. After World War II it more democratically became a 'beach for everyone', and now it can be crowded during the summer.

## GETTING THERE

Mondello is 11 km (7 miles) from Palermo (see map page 115). Regular bus services run from Palermo to Mondello, a half-hour trip. From Piazza Sturzo or Viale della Liberta in Palermo take bus no. 806, and in summer no. 833 also runs to the resort. The last bus leaves Mondello about 23.30, a taxi back to the city centre costs approximately €30.

### Tourist Office

The tourist kiosk (which open in summer only) is on the seafront and offers limited information.

## SIGHTS

This small fishing village on the shores of the turquoise Mediterranean Sea has a marvellous sandy beach that stretches

● *Mondello attracts sunbathers and sailors alike*

2 km (1.2 miles) opening onto a half-moon shaped bay between Monte Pellegrino and Monte Gallo. For centuries this seaside retreat has lured not only fishermen to its harbour full of fish, mussels, clams and octopus, but also visitors and Sicilians alike for the beach and the delicious, fresh seafood.

The beach, or lido, leads up to the town with its hotels, bars, cafes and nightclubs. Come in the daytime and you can divide your time between the beach, and eating on the seafront, a major occupation here.

● *Mondello's harbourside – pretty by day and lively by night*

## TAKING A BREAK/AFTER DARK

There's a line of trattorias along the seafront, some with outdoor
terraces where the fresh fish is displayed in boxes, and the lines of
patrons are long, particularly in summer. Your best bet for takeaway
food are the waterfront stalls, offering excellent Sicilian dishes such
as *pasta con le sarde* (pasta with olive oil and sardines), deep-fried
vegetables, shrimps and octopus.

At night, you can bar hop with the young, twenty-something,
crowd of Palermitani and visitors. Summer nights are lively and fun,
as Piazza Mondello is packed with people, cars with young locals
cruise the strip, and music pumps from the open-air discotheques.

# Monreale

Monreale, a small hill town 8 km (5 miles) south-west of Palermo commands unsurpassed views down the Conca d'Oro (Golden Shell) valley with the capital in the distance. The town grew up around the cathedral (Duomo) and the royal palace built by the Norman king, William II, in 1174. The life and soul of this old town still radiates around these buildings, surrounded by a myriad of tiny streets lined with shops, bars and restaurants.

## GETTING THERE

Monreale is a 20 minute bus ride on either bus 309 or 389, connecting the Piazza dell'Indipendenza with Monreale. The 389 bus drops you right in Piazza Monreale by the Duomo, the 309 leaves you in the centre of town, where it is a few minutes walk along the Corso Pietro Novelli and Via Roma up to the cathedral.

If arriving in Monreale by car from Palermo via the Viale Regional Siciliana, take the Calatafimi-Monreale exit and then follow N186.

### Tourist Office

Information is available from the tourist office in the cathedral square. ⏱ Mon–Sat 08.30–13.30, 14.30–18.30. ☎ 091.656.4501.

## SIGHTS & ATTRACTIONS

### The Duomo (Cathedral)

Legend has it the vision of the Duomo came to King William in a dream where the Madonna came to him saying that he should build a church with the treasure stolen from the state by his father,

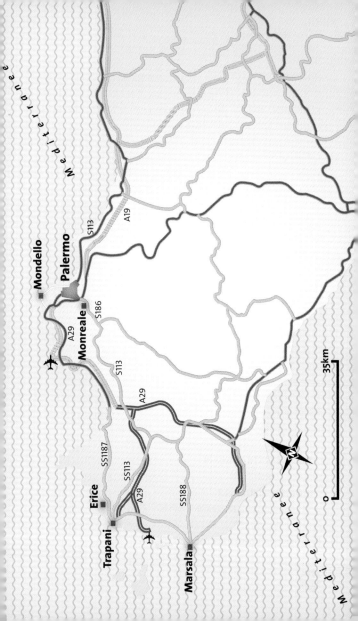

William I. She instructed him to make it so grandiose that it would rival the splendour of the Palatine Chapel in Palermo, built by his grandfather Roger II. To that endeavor William hired the most skilled craftsmen for the project, sparing no expense.

In 1174, at the young age of 20, William began construction of the cathedral, the Benedictine abbey, the Archbishop Palace and the Royal Palace. It was his ambition to hand down to posterity his own name and that of his royal Norman house by erecting a magnificent Christian church, a monumental architectural project to be a testimony to his Christian faith. He wanted to assume the title of Caliph under the name of 'al-Musta izz bi-llah' ('He who searches exultation in God'). The king was inspired of his profound religious faith by political and historical reasons of State.

The Latin basilican plan with the Byzantine-type cross plan is not domed and covers a vast area, 102 m (335 ft) long and 40 m (131 ft) wide. It is divided by 18 columns into a nave and aisles with capitals of exquisite workmanship, decorated with mosaic-covered *pulvinoes* (Byzantine transformation of the Greek *abacus*), *clypei* of pagan divinities, acanthus leaves and cornucopias overflowing with fruit.

The columns bear Saracen-style pointed arches; the granite floor, with porphyry geometric decorations, is the original one from the 16th century. The walls of nave, transept and apses are entirely decorated with mosaics on a gilded background, covering a total area of 6,340 sq m (7582 sq yds).

Although the cathedral is rather plain on the exterior, the glorious interior more than makes up for that. The mosaic decorations are the work of Byzantine and Venetian craftsmen, executed between the end of the 12th century and the beginning of

○ *Monreale's cathedral encloses a wealth of colourful mosaics*

the 13th century, and depict scenes from the Old and New Testaments. All the mosaics in the church were thought to have been completed in just ten years.

In the central apse your eyes are immediately drawn over the wooden ceiling to the mosaic figure of Christ in benediction, the face and shoulders alone are 20 m (66 ft) high, the outstretched arms and hands seem to be encompassing the beauty of the church. Underneath is a marvelous mosaic of the Virgin and Child attended to by angels and below this are the saints, each of whom are beautifully coloured and identified by name. Surprisingly, included in all this is the figure of Thomas Becket, marked 'SCS Thomas Cantb', he was canonised in 1173 just before the mosaics were begun. It is presumed that William included this as a political show of support for the papacy.

The two side apses are dedicated to Saint Peter on the right as you enter and Saint Paul on the left. The arches before each apse depict the martyrdom of each. The wonderful mosaics in the nave are an animated series that starts with the Creation above the pillars on the right of the altar, the scene continues on through the entire church. The darker aisle mosaics depict the teachings of Jesus, Adam and Eve, Abraham on the verge of sacrificing his son, and Noah's ark scenes showing the ship being built, animals being loaded aboard, Noah's family peering out of the hatches, as well as the Feeding of the Five Thousand and the Creation itself, gloriously simple panels showing God filling the world with animals, water, light and man.

It is difficult to keep your eyes off the mosaics, but be sure to allow time to explore the entire building. Above the two thrones are more mosaics; William receiving the crown from Christ and the king offering the cathedral to the Virgin. Both William I and William II are buried here in the side chapels; the cathedral's benefactor is in the white marble sarcophagus to the right of the apse.

Access to the tower is in the south-west corner of the cathedral, a climb of the 180 steps will bring you to the roof and magnificent views of the cloisters. If you are not bothered by heights you can walk around the outside of the church and upwards to the central apse. Once back inside you can purchase tickets for collection of the reliquaries in the treasury at the end of the left aisle.

🕐 Daily, 08.00–18.30, May–Oct; 08.00–12.30, 15.30–18.30, Nov–Apr. Treasure, daily 09.30–12.00, 15.30–18.00. Admission charged.

## The Apse and Cloisters

The cathedral's solid exterior merits a closer look, particularly the triple apse. The delicate polychromatic designs on the limestone and lava rock are quite exquisite. The apse is supported by slender columns and a series of delicate arches. To get the entire effect of the enormity and beauty of this you have to circle the cathedral by walking down a street to the left of the entrance.

It is worth visiting the Chiostro dei Benedettini, or, the cloisters, part of William's original Benedictine monastery. The garden is surrounded by 216 twin columns supporting pointed arches, a legacy of the Arab influence in Sicilian art. The carved capitals of the 12th-century columns depict various scenes; armed hunters doing battle with beasts, men lifting a casket of wine, and on others are flowers, birds, snakes and foliage. Enter the cloisters from Piazza Gugliemo, in the corner by the right-hand tower of the cathedral.

🕐 Cloisters, Mon–Sat 09.00–19.00, Sun 09.00–13.00. Admission charged.

**The rest of town**

Once you have seen the cathedral take a stroll through the dense latticework of steep, narrow streets. In little tucked away piazzas are several baroque churches, most of them locked, but one that you should be able to enter is the Chiese del Monte on Via Umberto,

inside are stuccos by Serpotta. Behind the cloisters is the new convent, built in 1747, the convent displays Pietro Novelli's wonderful 17th-century painting of St Benedict handing out bread to monks

*The impressive cloisters at Monreale cathedral*

and knights, from the grounds there are excellent views of the belvedere.

If you are interested in watching mosaic restorers at work there is the Instituto Statale d'Arte per il Mosaico near the Carabenieri barracks. Otherwise, it is easy to while away some time at any of the bars or trattorias in the Piazza Vittorio Emanuele.

## TAKING A BREAK

There's a good selection of places to eat in the streets just off the Piazza Duomo, though they can be pricey.

**Dietro L'Angolo €–€€** A two-minute walk from the Duomo towards the belvedere. Enjoy inexpensive Sicilian pasta dishes on the terrace with spectacular views. ❸ Via Piave 5.

**Mizzica €–€€** If you walk up towards the Duomo and head left down a street before reaching the apse you will come to Mizzica, a popular choice with tourists. ❸ Via Cappuccini 6.
🕑 Closed Tues.

**Trattoria da Peppino €–€€** Family-run trattoria offering decent meals and great pizzas. ❸ Along Via Roma from the Duomo and down a side street off Piazzetta Giuseppe Vaglica. 🕑 Closed Thurs.

**Bricco & Bacco €€** Standard brasserie cum wine bar offering an inexpensive menu. ❸ Via B. D'Acquisto 13.

**Taverna del Pavone €€** This informal restaurant has a friendly, easygoing atmosphere and serves typical Sicilian cuisine at

reasonable prices. 🄐 Vicolo Pensato 18. 🄣 091.640.6209.
🄔 bcec@libero.it 🄛 Closed Mon and 15–30 June.

## EVENTS & FESTIVALS

### Puppet Theatre

Sanicola Theatre offers puppet shows on summer evenings.
🄐 Via Benedetto 33. 🄣 091.640.9441. 🄛 Mon, Wed and Sat at 17.30
and 21.00. Admission charged.

**Festival of Sacred Music** (Settimana de Musica Sacra), takes place
between September and December with concerts of sacred,
spiritual and liturgical music held in the town's churches. For
information contact the tourist office 🄐 Zichichi, Via N. Nasi 27.

## ACCOMMODATION

There is limited accommodation in town. The following are two
options that are quite good and will not break your budget.

**Carrubella Park €–€€** Pleasant, family-run inn, close to everything.
🄐 Via Umberto 1. 🄣 091.640.2187.

**La Ciambra Bed & Breakfast €–€€** Wedged into a web of narrow
streets behind the Duomo's apse. Bright, clean, good value for
money. 🄐 Via Sanches 23. 🄣 091.640.9565. 🄦 www.laciambra.com

# Trapani & Marsala

Trapani, the ancient *Drepanon* (sickle), extends along a curving piece of land that ends in two tentacles jutting into the sea, one occupied by the Torre di Ligny built in 1671 as a defensive bastion, the other by a *lazaretto*, a house used for the treatment of lepers.

Legend has it that the coastline was formed by the sickle that was dropped by the goddess of agriculture, Demeter (Ceres) while she desperately sought her daughter Persephone, who had been carried off by Hades. The northern edge of the coastline provides protected anchorages and moorings for fishing boats. The well-protected harbour handles large consignments of salt gathered in the salt pans just south of the town and tuna fish processed at the local canning factory. Each morning on the shore opposite the harbour a lively and boisterous fish market is held.

Trapani (see map, page 115) is the first of three major towns on Sicily's western edge (Erice and Marsala being the other two). Although it is mostly modern, Trapani's old centre – on a narrow arm of land pointing out into the sea – is elegant. The town's rather plain monuments give no hint to its long and impressive history.

Trapani profited by its position looking out towards Africa. It was a stopover on sea routes linking Tunis, Naples, Anjou and Aragon, a role it played throughout the Middle Ages when European royalty passed each other on the quayside. The Navarrese king Theobald died here in 1270; in 1272 Edward I of England landed here after a crusade to learn that he had inherited the throne. Peter of Aragon arrived in 1282 to claim the Sicilian throne after the expulsion of the Angevin French.

The most exciting time to visit is over Easter when the old town is thronged with crowds of people participating in the processions and festivities of Holy Week, the celebrations culminate on Good Friday with the *Processione dei Misteri*, when 20 groups of sculpted figures, dating back to 1650, are borne through the streets all day and night by, as Sicilian tradition mandates, men from various church associations.

Marsala is an excellent day or overnight trip. Besides being world famous for its wine, the town has an interesting history.

The Carthaginians founded the town on Cape Lilibeo (now called Cape Boeo) in 396 BC after fleeing nearby Motya, which had been destroyed by armies of Syracusans, they named it Lilybaeum. It fell to the Romans in 241 BC and saw the arrival of Julius Caesar in 47 BC when he was enroute to North Africa. It was while under the rule of the Saracens that the name was changed to Marsa el Allah, meaning port of God.

The town scored its place in modern Italian history for its role in the story of the Risorgimento, the struggle for Italian unity in the 19th century. It was from here that Garibaldi started his campaign to drive out the Bourbons, in the company of his red shirted 'Thousand'. You can see memorials to Garibaldi, the hero of Sicily, in street names and statuary. One of prominence is the Porto Garibaldi, at the end of Via Garibaldi, which recounts the hero's entry into Marsala. Each year on 11 May local enthusiasts in red shirts gather here to re-enact the exploits of Garibaldi's 'Thousand'.

## GETTING THERE

### TRAPANI

Trapani is approximately 100 km (62 miles) south-west of Palermo, reachable by bus or train, 3 hr 30 min and 2 hrs respectively. The bus and train stations are both located in Piazza Umberto I. For further information and timetables contact Autoservizi Segesta bus ( 092.321.754) or for FS train network go to  www.trenitalia.it. Or contact the main tourist office in Palermo or the office in Trapani.

## MARSALA

The town is 31 kms (19 miles) south of Trapani, 124 km (77 miles) south-west of Palermo,

Marsala's rail station is at the southeastern edge of town on Via A. Fazio, a 15 minute walk from the centre. Buses arrive centrally at Piazza del Popolo (also known as Piazza Marconi) near Porto Garibaldi. By train or bus, Marsala is 90 mins from Palermo, 45 mins from Trapani.

The ancient city of Trapani juts into the Mediterranean sea

**Tourist Offices**

**Trapani** ❷ Piazzeta Saturno. ☎ 092.329.000.

**Marsala** ❸ Via XI Maggio 100, off Piazza Repubblica near the Chiesa
Madre. ☎ 092.371.4097. Most of the town's tourist sites have notices
posted in English.

## SIGHTS & ATTRACTIONS

### TRAPANI

Almost everything of interest in Trapani is found in the old town,
which is about a 15 minute walk west from the train station.
Although there has been some restoration of churches and palaces
over the years, off the main corso and away from the central
shopping areas there is a derelict and scruffy look to the city with
litter covered streets and palazzi allowed to crumble from years of

accumulated grime.

You will not see any of this if you stick to the Corso Vittorio Emanuele, the old town's pedestrianised main street that is dominated at its eastern end by the pink marble front of the Palazzo Senatorio, the 17th-century town hall. With its twin clocks separated by an elegant eagle the building adds a bit of grandeur to the thin promenading strip hemmed in by balconied palazzi and some baroque churches, the best of which is the Cattedral of San Lorenzo.

## Centro Storico

The medieval district of the old town is situated on the headland pointing out to sea. The tip was developed by the Spanish in the 14th century (Quartiere Palazzo), and remodeled in the baroque style several centuries later. The oldest section was built in true Moorish fashion around a tight network of interconnecting narrow streets that originally would have been enclosed by walls.

## Rua Nova

Now called Via Garibaldi the Aragonese laid the 'new road' in the 13th century. In the 18th century aristocrats built their palazzis and churches along it; Palazzo Riccio di Morana, Palazzo Milo and Badia Nuova (Santa Maria del Soccorso), whose interior is highly decorated with baroque polychrome marble and contains several elaborate galleries.

🅐 Badia Nuova. 🕐 daily 08.15–13.00, ☎ 092.343.2111.

## Via Torrearsa

Back at the eastern end of the Corso Vittorio Emanuele, Via Torrearsa is one of the old town's main shopping streets. At the northern end is an excellent daily morning market in the Piazza Mercato di Pesce; fish, fruit, vegetables, breads, local tuna products, olives and cheeses are on sale here, and many can be sampled.

## Rua Grande

Constructed in the 13th century this is Trapani's second main street (Corso Vittorio Emanuele was the first); lining it are elegant baroque palazzis – at number 86 are the Palazzo Berardo Ferro and the Sede del Vescovado (Bishop's Palace).

## The Cattedrale

This 17th-century cathedral is dedicated to Saint Lawrence. Its marvelous baroque exterior porticos and cupolas, along with the gigantic interior, have been restored in recent years to their original sandy hue. Inside is a Crucifixion attributed to Van Dyke.
ⓐ Via Corso Vittorio Emanuele. ① 092.323.362. ⓛ Mon–Fri 09.00–12.00, 17.00–18.00, Sat 09.00–12.00, Sun and public holidays. Donations welcome.

## Sant'Agostino

Built by the Knights Templar in the 14th century, the church was heavily damaged during World War II. The beautiful rose window of interlocking stone bands is original. The church is occasionally used as a concert hall; enquire at the tourist office for details on performances.
ⓐ Piazzetta Saturno, next to the tourist office.

## Biblioteca Fardelliana

Located near the church of Sant'Angelo this small museum has engravings from the Gatto collection, including views of the Trapani

area from the 17th to 20th centuries. ☎ 092.321.506. 🕐 July–Sept, 09.00–13.30; Aug 10.00–13.00; Oct–Jun, Mon–Fri 09.00–13.30, 15.00–19.30, Sat 09.00–13.30, closed Sun, public holidays and 7 Aug.

## Santa Maria di Gesu

Architecturally more appealing than Sant'Angelo is the 16th-century church of Santa Maria di Gesu. The Catalan doorway displays a diversity characteristic of Trapani, the right-hand one is Gothic, the other defiantly Renaissance, and there is a good relief in the architrave. Inside, at the end of the nave, is a terracotta Madonna degli Angeli designed by Andrea della Robbia, it is sheltered beneath a graceful marble canopy carved by Antonello Gagini. ❸ Via San Pietro. ☎ 092.387.2021. 🕐 Mon–Fri 07.30–10.00, Thur 17.00–18.00. Closed public holidays.

There is little else to see in this part of town except for the 16th-century Palazzo della Giudecca located on the street that bares its name. The stand-out architectural points on this palazzo are the plaque-studded facade and the Spanish-style windows. The building is in the heart of Trapani's old Jewish quarter, an area dating from the city's medieval days when it was the centre of Mediterranean trade. From here it is a short distance to the Villa Margherita, the beautiful, shady town gardens that are open from dawn to dusk. Concerts are held here on summer evenings.

## The Santuario dell'Annunziata

The only reason to go to the modern city is to visit Trapani's most lavishly decorated monument the Santaurio dell'Annunziata, a 14th-century Carmelite convent and church whose cloisters hold the town's main museum. The church was built in the 14th century and was enlarged in 1760 and, unfortunately, only the facade, with its

Gothic portal and rose-coloured window, is original.

The interior holds a several magnificent chapels, two are dedicated to Trapani's fishermen and seamen, one chapel carries the facade's shell motif design around the entire wall space.

Extending from behind the main altar of the chapel is the magnificent Cappella della Madonna; entrance is gained through a Renaissance arch designed in the 16th century by the Gagini family. The delicate bronze gates date back to 1591. On the altar is Trapani's sacred idol, the statue of a smiling Madonna and Child, attributed to Nino Pisano in the 14th century. Over the Madonna is an ostentatious marble canopy sculpted by Antonino Gagini, it is surrounded by polychrome marble. ⓐ Via Pepoli. ⓘ 092.353.9184. ⓛ Summer 07.00–12.00, 16.00–18.00; winter 07.00–10.00 and 16.00–19.00; Sun 07.00–13.30, 16.00–19.00. Donations welcome. ⓝ Bus 24, 25 or 30 from Piazza Vittorio Emanuele and get off at the park, Villa Pepoli, which is in front of the building.

## The Museo Regionale Pepoli

Adjacent to the Santuario dell'Annunziata the museum is housed in the former Carmelite convent. In a sumptuous setting there is a wide collection of archeological finds, sculpture and Sicilian paintings from the 12th through to the 18th centuries, and a large collection of Trapani art that includes coral carvings and jewellery. The most important works are; the pieces of Gagini statuary, a bronze horse and rider by Giacomo Serpotta, a 16th-century marble doorway by Berrettaro Bartolomeu, a Pieta by Roberto Oderisio and an 18th-century majolica-tiled scene of La Mattanza (tuna slaughter) with the fishermen depicted corralling and hauling the fish into their boat. ⓐ Via Conte Agostino Pepoli 200, the main entrance is through the Villa Pepoli. ⓘ 092.355.3269.

ℹ 092.353.5444. 🕐 Tues–Sun 09.00–13.30, festivals and holidays 09.00–12.30. Closed Mon.

### En route to Marsala

To get out and explore the surrounding area, it would be best to hire a car. In Nubia, approximately 6 km (4 miles) south in the direction of Marsala on the Provincial Road SP 21, are two sites that reflect Trapani's history in the salt industry; the Saline Nature Reserve and the Museo del Sale. The road skirts around the edge of a lagoon and provides fine views of the local salt works, panels of shimmering water strategically laid out and separated by thin strips of earth.

Trapani has been known as the salt capital of Italy since the days when it was under Phoenician control. It was the Phoenicians who built the original basins and windmills to collect the salt, which they then exported all over the Mediterranean. The Normans continued

the industry, the salt is still being extracted today although the methods used and the efforts expended have changed as processes have become mechanised. The picturesque windmills lining the roads are still used to pump seawater from one basin to the other. And even though automation has come to the region you can see bare-chested men toiling with shovels, carting full wheelbarrows across the pans to a conveyor belt which dumps 2 m (6.5 ft) high mounds of white salt along the banks of the saltpans.

### Riserva Naturale Salina de Trapani e Paceco (Saline Nature Reserve)

A saltwater nature reserve habitat where 170 species of birds, both resident and migratory, have been recorded. You can view flamingos, storks, cranes and herons.

⬇ *The importance of the salt industry to this area is readily apparent*

⊙ Via Garibaldi. ☎ 092.386.7700. ⊛ www.salineditrapani.it
🕐 09.00–18.00 (17.00 Oct–Mar), closed 25 Nov and public holidays.

## Museo del Sale di Nubia (Saline Museum of Nubia)

This small interesting salt museum has been set up in a 300-year-old salt worker's house. It tells and shows the different stages involved in harvesting salt from the saltpans. Among the displays are various special tools used in the extraction and harvest, including mill gearing, windmill vanes, cogwheels, spikes and sprockets. There are photographs of salt workers in action that help to clarify the work involved in the process. ⊙ Via Garibaldi. ☎ 092.386.7142, Mon–Sat 09.30–13.00, 15.30–18.30 (15.00 in winter), Sun 09.30–13.00. Thirty-minute guided tours available. Audio-visual presentation. Admission charged.

## MARSALA

The heart of Marsala is Piazza della Repubblica in the town centre, surrounded by a baroque assortment of buildings and narrow traffic free streets.

## Chiesa Madre

This 18th-century church is dedicated to San Tommaso di Canterbury, patron saint of Marsala. In contrast to the elegant baroque exterior, the rather disappointing interior is dark and gloomy, but, does hold a number of interesting Gagini sculptures. ⊙ Piazza della Repubblica. 🕐 Daily 0.800–17.00.

## Museo degli Arazzi

Located behind the chiesa the only display at the museo is a collection of eight enormous hand stitched wool and silk tapestries depicting the capture of Jerusalem. Made in Brussels in the sixteenth century, they are beautifully turned out in burnished red, gold and green. ❸ Via Garraffa 57. ⏰ Tues–Sun 09.00–1300 and 16.00–18.00. Admission charged.

## Insula Romana

Make your way up from Piazza della Repubblica to Via XI Maggio, lined with upscale shops, pretty courtyards, and cafés. At the far end of Via XI Maggio, through the 18th-century Porta Nuova, on the Piazza della Vittoria is the municipal gardens, beyond the piazza lies Capo Boeo, the westernmost point of Sicily that was the first settlement of the survivors of annihilated Motya. All the town's major antiquities are here, including the old Insula Romana, housed here is most of what has been excavated so far of the old city of Lilybaeum. Most of it is from the 3rd century BC Roman, as you might guess from the presence of the vomitorium, lodged in one entire section of the site, the edificio termale, or bathhouse. There is some wonderful mosaicwork here; a chained dog at the entrance and a hunting scene in the atrium.

From Piazza della Vittoria, Viale N. Sautro leads to the church of San Giovanni, under which is a grotto reputed to have been inhabited by the sibyl Lilibetana, endowed with paranormal gifts. There's another slice of mosaic here, and a well whose water is meant to impart second sight.

## Museo Archeologico

Behind the church, in one of the stone vaulted warehouses that line the promenade is the Museo Marsala, most of whose space is given over to a well preserved exhibit of a warship from the classical period. Displayed in a heat and humidity regulated plastic tent, it

ranks as the only existing liburnian, a specifically Phoenician or Punic warship, probably sunk during the First Punic War in the great sea battle off the Egadi Islands that ended Carthage's rule of the waves. Brought here in 1977 after eight years of underwater surveying by a British team working under the archaeologist Honor Frost, the vessel, originally 35 m (115 ft) long and rowed by 68 oarsmen, has been a fount of information on the period, including what the crew ate. Throughout the rest of the museum are items found in or around the ship.

Viale N. Sauro (behind the church of San Giovanni).

Mon, Tues and Thurs 09.00–13.30, Wed, Fri, Sat and Sun 16.00–19.00. Admission charged

## CAFES & RESTAURANTS

### TRAPANI

Eating out in Trapani is a very pleasant experience even if most of the restaurants and trattorrias do not have outdoor seating. What makes it special is the food, fresh fish and couscous is served almost everywhere, be sure and try a local pasta speciality *alla Trapanese*, is terrific – either spaghetti or home-made *busiate* pasta served with a pesto of fresh tomato, basil, garlic and almonds, sometime accompanied by fried potatoes.

**Calvino €** Serves superb hot pizza. Try a local speciality – the Rianata, made with fresh oregano, tomato, garlic, anchovies and pecorino cheese. Via N. Nasi 7. 092.321.464.

**Ai Lumi €€** A favourite with the locals this taverna serves regional dishes, such as *ghiotta di pesce* (seafood soup), home made pasta,

grilled meats and fish. ❷ Corso Vittorio Emanuele 75.
❶ 092.387.2418. ◐ Closed Sun.

**La Bettolacca €€** Friendly, informal osteria known for its excellent
risotto, pasta and fish dishes such as oven-baked *bucatini* (like
hollow spaghetti) with sardines. ❷ Via General Enrico Fardella 25.
Located just off the corso, around the corner from the Messina hotel
(see page 138). ❶ 092.321.695.

**P&G €€€** A smart restaurant with a great chef who prepares a
fantastic antipasto selection, excellent grilled fish and *spaghetti alla
Trapanese* with fried potatoes and served with anchovy, garlic, pine
nuts and tomato. ❷ Via Spalti 1. ❶ 092.354.7701. ◐ Closed Sun.

### MARSALA

In the centre, which empties of life after 21.00, restaurants can be
hard to come by. The couple of bars in Piazza della Repubblica are
good for a *te freddo alla pesca* (peach tea) and loud discussions
about the lottery numbers. After dinner, finish off with a beer or an
ice cream at one of the cafes outside Porta Nuova, where you can sit
and admire the austere art deco front of the Cine Impero, so out of
keeping with the baroque arch opposite. To sample some marsala
wine visit either the **Enoteca Sombrero** (❷ Via Garibaldi 32) or one of
two adjacent enoteca-souvenir shops in Via Lungomare Boeo, by the
archeological museum.

**Caffe Millennium €–€€** This is the best place for breakfast, and,
handy for anyone staying at the President or Garden hotels. Offers
grilled sandwiches and good coffee, lunch specials and it stays open
late on the weekends. ❷ Piazza F. Pizzo.

**Capo Lilybeo €–€€** In a restored warehouse near the archeological museum. The food here is terrific – try the *busiate alla Marsigliese* (with shrimp and lobster ragu), and it also known for its fish couscous (served on Fridays). ❷ Via Lungomare Boeo 40. ❶ 092.317.2881.

**Tratorria Garibaldi €€–€€€** Cosy, upmarket trattoria in the centre. Fish is the speciality, though you will eat for less if you choose the grilled meat. ❷ Piazza Addolorata 5. ❶ 092.395.3006.

## ACCOMMODATION

### TRAPANI

Trapani's cheaper accommodation options are all in the old town. With the exception of Easter time, finding a place to stay is generally not a problem.

**Ostello per la Gioventu €** The only youth hostel in the area, it is hidden away 3 km (2 miles) out of town and open only after 18.00 each day. ❷ Contrada Raganzili. ❶ 092.355.2964. ❷ Take bus no. 21 from the station or bus no. 23 from Piazza Vittorio Emanuele II, a 15-minute ride and get off at Ospedale Villa dei Gerani, from the stop take the second street on the right and walk 600 m (656 yds) uphill.

**Messina €** Occupying the first floor of the 18th-century Palazzo Bernardo Ferro, it shares the courtyard with Ai Lumi (see page 140). The rooms are not impressive and some of the staff smoke, but it is cheap and clean. Advance reservations suggested. Shared bathrooms. ❷ Corso Vittorio Emanuele 71. ❶ 092.321.198.

## A HISTORY OF MARSALA WINE

The Baglio Anselmi, in which Marsala's archeological museum is housed, is one of a number of old *bagli*, or warehouse, conspicuous throughout this wine making region. Many are still used in the making of the famous dessert wine that carries the town's name. It was Englishman John Woodhouse who first exploited the commercial potential of marsala wine, when he visited the town in 1770. Woodhouse realised that the local wine could travel for long periods without going off when fortified with alcohol. Others followed, including Ingham, Whittaker and Hopps, whose names can still be seen on some of the warehouse doors. It was the English presence in Marsala that persuaded Garibaldi to launch his campaign here as he judged that the Bourbon fleet would not dare to interfere close to Her Majesty's commercial concerns.

Marsala owes much of its current prosperity to the marketing of its wine, still a thriving industry, though no longer in British hands. You can visit some of the *bagli* and sample the wine for free: try the Stabilimento Florio (🕒 Mon – Fri 10.00–13.00, 15.30–18.00. ☎ 092.396.9667 to arrange a guided tour), located on Lungomare Mediterraneo, to the south of town beyond the port. There is an Enomuseum (🕒 daily 08.30–13.00, 15.00–19.00, free) at Contrada Berbaro (3 km along the road to Mazara del Vallo) where you can look over the old apparatus used for wine making. Otherwise, you will find marsala or the sweeter *marsala all'uovo* (mixed with egg yolks) in every bar and restaurant in town.

**Ai Lumi €€** This small bed and breakfast has five small pristine rooms and apartments, and a good trattoria a few doors down from it. ❸ Corso Vittorio Emanuele 71. ☎ 092.387.2418.

**Maccotta €€** Clean and friendly place behind the Palazzo Senatorio that has spacious modern rooms, the cheapest of which share a bathroom. ❸ Via degri Argentieri 4. ☎ 092.328.418 or 092.343.7693. @ albergo-maccotta@comeg.it

**Nuovo Russo €€** Best choice in the old town for comfort and moderate prices. Tile-floored rooms are clean and bright with good bathrooms. Front rooms face the cathedral and have small terraces overlooking the corso. Breakfast and air-conditioning available for an extra charge. ❸ Via Tintori 4. ☎ 092.211.166 or 092.326.623.

## MARSALA

**Garden €** The cheapest hotel in town, nine rooms, behind the rail station. Modern and clean. ❸ Via Gambini 36. Right over the train level crossing, then right again. ☎ 092.398.2320.

**Villa Favorita €–€€** This beautiful, secluded villa is set in its own gardens and has a pool and a charming restaurant. It is 2 km (1.2 miles) from the centre and is well signposted. ❸ Via Favorita. ☎ 092.398.9100. ⊕ 092.398.0264.

**President €€€** Spacious rooms, comfortable beds in this solid business hotel. Swimming pool. Twenty minute walk from the centre. ❸ Via Nino Bixio. ☎ 092.399.9333. ⊕ 092.399.9115.

---

● *Calling from a card phone may be cheaper than using your mobile*

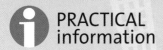

# PRACTICAL
# information

# Directory

### GETTING THERE

The best and least expensive means of travel to Palermo is either by air or rail. If you want to arrive by sea, an alternative would be to book a budget flight from the UK to mainland Italy that can be combined with ferry services to Palermo (see By sea page 50).

### By air

Budget airlines have made it possible to fly direct from the UK to Palermo much easier and cheaper. No frills are offered, but the savings can be quite substantial.

Fares depend on what season you choose to travel, the highest being at Easter, anytime between June and mid-August and around Christmas. Prices are considerably lower during September to October, November to March and April to May.

### Booking flights online

Four main online booking sites are Expedia (🖢 www.expedia.co.uk), Orbitz (🖢 www.orbitz.com), Priceline (🖢 www.priceline.com) and Travelocity (🖢 www.travelocity.com).

### Flights

Airlines in the UK, Ireland and Italy that offer flights between these countries are:

**Aer Lingus** UK: ☎ 0845 084 4444. Republic of Ireland ☎ 0818.365.0000. 🖢 www.aerlingus.ie

**Air Berlin** UK: ☎ 0870 738 8880. 🖢 www.airberlin.com

**Air Malta** UK: ☎ 0845 607 3710. 🖢 www.airmalta.com

**Alitalia** UK: ☎ 0870 544 8259. 🖢 www.alitalia.co.uk

**British Airways** UK: ☎ 0870 850 9850. Republic of Ireland:
☎ 1 800 616 747. ⓦ www.britishairways.com
**easyJet** UK: ☎ 0871 750 0100. ⓦ www.easyjet.com
**Hapag-Lloyd Express** UK: ☎ 0870 606 0519.
ⓦ www.hapaglloydexpress.com
**Meridiana** UK: ☎ 0207 730 3454. ⓦ www.meridiana.it
**Ryanair** UK: ☎ 0871 246 0000. Republic of Ireland: ☎ 0818 303 030.
ⓦ www.ryanair.com
**Volare** UK: ☎ 0800 032 0992. Outside UK 44.207.365.8235.
ⓦ www.volareweb.com

Airlines in the USA and Canada
**Air Canada** ☎ 1 888 247 2262. ⓦ www.aircanada.ca
**American Airlines** ☎ 1 800 433 7300. ⓦ www.aa.com
**British Airways** USA & Canada. ☎ 1.800.AIRWAYS.
ⓦ www.britishairways.com
**Delta Airlines** ☎ 800 241 4141. ⓦ www.delta.com
**Iberia** ☎ 1 800 772 4642. ⓦ www.iberia.com
**KLM/Northwest** ☎ 1 800 447 4747. ⓦ www.klm.com
**Lufthansa** USA: ☎ 1 800 645 3880. Canada ☎ 1 800 563 5954.
ⓦ www.lufthansia.ca.com
**SAS Scandinavian Airlines** ☎ 1 800 221 2350. ⓦ www.flysas.com.

### By rail

The long train ride south through Italy is a popular way to go
(see page 49), allowing stop-offs at various locations before
reaching Palermo. The Europe wide InterRail and Eurail passes
give unlimited travel on the FS network. The monthly *Thomas Cook
European Timetable* has up-to-date schedules for european and
italian services.

**Thomas Cook European Rail Timetable** ☎ (UK) 01733 416477; (USA) 1 800 322 3834. 🌐 www.thomascookpublishing.com

**Rail ticket agencies**

UK and Ireland

**Eurostar** ☎ 0870 518 6186. 🌐 www.eurostar.co.uk

**Italian State Railways** ☎ 0207 724 0011. 🌐 www.fs-on-line.com

**Rail Europe** ☎ 0870 584 8848. 🌐 www.raileurope.co.uk

**Travel Cuts** ☎ 0207 255 1944. 🌐 www.travelcuts.co.uk

US and Canada

**CIT Rail** US: ☎ 1 800 223 7987 or 1.800.CIT.TOUR. Canada: ☎ 1 800 387 0711. 🌐 www.fs-on-line.com and www.cit-tours.com

**DER Travel** US: ☎ 1.800.782.2424. 🌐 www.dertravel.com/Rail

**Europrail International Inc**. Canada: ☎ 1.888.667.9734. www.europrail.net

**Eurail** US: ☎ 1.800.438.7245. Canada: ☎ 1.800.361.7245. 🌐 www.raileurope.com/us

Australia and New Zealand

**CIT World Travel** Australia ☎ 02.9267.1255. 🌐 www.cittravel.com.au

### TRAVEL INSURANCE

However you book your city break, it is important to take out adequate personal travel insurance for the trip. For peace of mind the policy should give cover for medical expenses, loss, theft, repatriation, personal liability and cancellation expenses. If you are hiring a vehicle you should also check that you are appropriately insured and make sure that you take relevant insurance documents and your driving licence with you.

**Rail Plus** Australia ☎ 1300.555.003 or 03.9642.8644. New Zealand: ☎ 09.303.2484. 🌐 www.railplus.com.au

**Trailfinders** Australia ☎ 1300.780.212. 🌐 www.trailfinders.com.au

## ENTRY FORMALITIES

### Documentation

It is now mandatory that you show photo identification along with your ticket, before you will be allowed to board your flight(s).

UK, Irish and other European Union (EU) citizens can enter Sicily and stay as long as they want by producing a valid passport. Citizens of the United States, Canada, Australia and New Zealand need only a valid passport, but are limited to stays of three months. All other nationals should consult the relevant embassies about visa or passport requirements.

You are required to register with the local police within three days of arriving in Italy; if you are staying at a hotel and have presented your passport this will be done for you. Don't be surprised if you do go to the local police station to register and nobody there knows what you are talking about as hardly any visitors comply with this law.

Nationals of the European Union intending to drive a car in the country require a valid national driving licence. Nationals of non EU countries should obtain an international driving licence, which can be obtained in the US from the American Automobile Association. The AAA can be contacted at AAA National Headquarters, 🏢 1000 AAA Drive, Heathrow, FL 32746; ☎ 407.444.7000, 🌐 www.aaa.com. You must be over 18 years of age to drive a car in Italy.

### Customs

EU citizens can bring goods for personal use when arriving from another EU country, but must observe the limits on tobacco (800 cigarettes) and spirits (10 litres over 22 per cent alcohol, 90 litres of wine). Limits for non-EU nationals are 200 cigarettes and one litre of spirits, two of wine.

## MONEY

Italy's currency is the euro, notes are issued in denominations of 5, 10, 20, 50, 100, 200, and 500 euros. Coins are issued in denominations of 1, 2, 5, 10, 20, and 50 cents and 1 and 2 euros.

It is a good idea to have some cash on hand when you first arrive. You should be able to order euro notes from your bank, or from branches of Thomas Cook and American Express. You will find ATM's and money exchange bureaux at the airport and around Palermo.

The easiest way not to deal with the exchange is by using your credit or debit card. Before leaving home check with your bank to make sure that your personal identification number gives you access to ATMs/cashpoint machines (*bancomat*) abroad. The cards can be used at hotels, restaurants, some shops and for cash advances. Be aware that in the high season it is not unusual for machines to run out of cash, so keep some in reserve.

It's always a good idea to have some travellers' cheques on hand when you travel. Try to get them in different denominations and keep a record of the cheques serial numbers in a different place from the actual cheques. On euro travellers' cheques you should not have to pay any commission when exchanging them in Palermo for euros. For other currency cheques there is usually a commission charge of one percent of the amount changed.

### Money Wiring

This is never a convenient or cheap experience, but if the need arises for you to have money wired use one of the companies listed below.

It is also possible to have money wired directly from your bank at home to a bank in Palermo. This process takes two business days and there is a charge involved.

**Travellers Express/Moneygram** UK, Ireland and New Zealand: ☎ 0800.6663.9472. US: ☎ 1.800.444.3010. Canada: ☎ 1.800.933.3278. Australia: ☎ 001.1.800.6663.9472. 🌐 www.moneygram.com

**Western Union** UK: ☎ 0800 833 833. Republic of Ireland: ☎ 66.947.5603. 🌐 www.westernunion.com.US and Canada: ☎ 1.800.CALL.CASH. Australia: ☎ 1.800.501.500. New Zealand: ☎ 0.800.005.253. Customers in the US and Canada can send money online.

## HEALTH, SAFETY & CRIME

Subjects of the European Union will require an EHIC (European Health Insurance Card) to obtain free medical treatment. As an EU country Italy has free reciprocal health agreements with other member states, but even if you are covered under this you should make sure you have travel insurance that includes a medical policy. Keep any bills incurred if you will be seeking reimbursement.

In the event that you have anything stolen you must obtain an official statement from the police, not an easy thing to do in Sicily but be persistent as without it you will not be able to get claim your loss to the insurance company.

Vaccinations are not required though it is always a good idea to be up to date with tetanus and Hepatitis B shots. The water is safe to drink, but as the taste leaves something to be desired, stay with bottled water, *aqua minerale*, which is inexpensive and readily available. In public fountains be on the lookout for '*aqua non potable*' signs, which means the water is not safe to drink.

Pharmacists (*farmacia*) are qualified to give you medical advice and dispense prescriptions. Generally one pharmacy stays open all night in each quarter of Palermo. You can locate the name and number of the pharmacy that is open late or all night on any *farmacia* door or listed in the local paper.

If you don't have a spare pair of glasses take a copy of your prescription with you, as an optician, *ottico*, should be able to make you a new pair if yours are lost or damaged.

### Crime

Petty juvenile crime is rampant in Palermo. Gangs of *scippatori* or bag snatchers strike in crowded streets, marketplaces and parks. Whether on foot or riding scooters they act fast, disappearing before you have had time to react. It is not only handbags they are after, they can whip wallets out of your pocket without your knowing it and tear off visible jewellery and cameras.

Do not flash around large sums of money, leave all jewellery at home, keep a firm grip on cameras, carry your handbag across your body and in front of you, put your wallet in your front pocket, or use a body wallet that you wear either around your waist or your neck under your clothing. Avoid dark streets and alleys. If you find you are out late at night swallow the expense and take a taxi back to your accommodation.

In the event of theft you will need to report it at the *Questera*, the headquarters of the *Polizia Statale*. Find the address in the local *Tuttocitta* magazine or ask at your hotel. If you have to deal with the police be prepared for a lot of frustration and piles of paperwork.

### OPENING HOURS

Most shops and businesses are open Monday to Saturday from 09.00 to 13.00 and 16.00 to 20.00. Everything, except bars and restaurants, closes on Sundays. The main banks in Palermo are the Banco di Sicilia, the Banca Populare Sant'Angelo, the Cassa di Risparmio, the Banca Nuova and the Banca Nazionale di Lavoro. Their banking hours are Mon–Fri 08.30–13.20 and 15.00–16.00.

Pharmacies are closed at night though one in each district remains open late. In August many stores and shops are closed in the afternoons. Some close completely the first two weeks of August.

Except for the Feast of Saint Rosalia on 15 July (see page 10), shops and businesses do not close for religious holidays. Bars and restaurants are open on public holidays, everything else is closed.

Museums are open Tuesday–Saturday from 09.00–13.00 with some open in the afternoons from 16.00–19.00. Archeological sites are open Monday–Friday from 09.00–12.00 and 16.00–19.00 and Saturday 09.00–12.00; summer hours may be longer.

Churches are open in the morning from 07.00–12.00 and again in the afternoons from 16.00–19.00. Smaller ones might only be open for early morning and evening services and some open only on Sundays and religious holidays. When visiting a church always dress appropriately.

Closed for restorations (*chiuso per restauro*) is a sign that you will see on many churches, convents, and oratories – even if there is scaffolding and work going on, have a try at persuading a workman, curator or priest to show you around.

## TOILETS

The signs for women's toilets are *Donne* or *Signore*, while men's facilities will be marked *Uomini* or *Signori*. Public toilets are not easy to find other than at tourist sights and stations, so bars and cafés are the best bet, though you would be expected to buy a drink in these establishments.

## CHILDREN

Pharmacies and supermarkets carry most baby products, everything from nappies to formula to baby food. Restaurants generally do not offer a children's menu but most will provide a smaller version of an adult meal. Hotels charge extra to put an additional bed in the room. Generous discounts apply to children at most sites and attractions and when travelling on trains. There is plenty to keep children entertained in Palermo. Here is a selection.

● **Puppets, puppets and more puppets** Kids adore Palermo's Museo Internazionale delle Marionette (International Puppet Museum; see page 102). Sicilians call their famous puppets *pupi*, and they are truly works of folkloric art. In summer (July–Sept) free puppet shows are staged here, contact the museum (🕿 091.328.060) for dates and times of events. Puppet shows are also presented at Teatro Ippogrifo 🖈 Vicolo Ragusi 4. 🕿 091.329.194. 🚌 bus 225 🕒 daily at 17.30 (Sept–June) only.

● **A green spot** Away from the traffic and noise Palermo's public parks offer wonderful interludes for families. Especially inviting are the landscaped oases of Villa Giulia and, around the corner, the Orto Botanico, offering amenities such as a children's train, play area, bandstands, deer and ducks. Orto Botanico & Villa Giulia 🖈 Via Abramo Lincoln 28. 🕿 091.623.8241 🕒 08.00–dusk Admission charged. 🚌 Buses 139, 211, 221, 224, 226 or 227.

● **A day at the beach** Escape the city and head for Mondello Lido (see page 110) with its long, sandy beaches, shallow calm waters and plenty of pizza palaces to bring the kids to when they get hungry. 🚌 Bus 806 or 833 from Piazza Sturzo or Viale della Liberta.

- **Take a hike** See where sacred bones were found. The Riserva Monte Pellegrino Naturale (Monte Pellegrino Natural Reserve). Monte Pellegrino was occupied as far back as 7000 BC: Paleolithic incised drawings were found in the Grotto d'Addaura on Pellegrino's northern slopes and casts of these are in Palermo's Museo Archeologico (Archeological Museum). Today the mountain is used by picnickers and pilgrims here to visit the shrine of the city's patron saint, St Rosalia, William II's pious niece Rosalia renounced worldly possessions and fled to the mountain in 1159, and nothing was heard from her until the early 17th century, when her bones were discovered on Pellegrino. Pronounced sacred relics, the bones were paraded around the city in a successful attempt to stay the ravages of a terrible plague, a ceremony that is recreated every July 15th and September 4th with a torchlight procession to the saint's sanctuary.

  The half-hour ride to the mountain is beautiful, offering wide views over Palermo. You enter the Santuario di Santa Rosalia (🕐 daily 07.00–19.00) through a small chapel, built over a deep cave in the hillside where the bones of Rosalia were discovered in 1624. Inside is a reclining golden statue of the saint. A road to the left of the chapel leads up to the cliff-top promontory, a half-hour's walk, where a statue of St Rosalia stares out over the sprawling city below. Another path, leading up from the Santuario to the right, takes you to the top of the mountain, 600m (437 yds) high, a 40-minute walk. Other trails that cover the mountain are dotted with families picnicking and children playing. Riserva Monte Pellegrino Naturale, 🛈 091.671.6066 🚌 Bus 812 from Piazza Sturzo or Piazza Politeama.

## COMMUNICATIONS

### Phones

The telephone service is organised by Telecom Italia. Each office has public booths where the customer pays for units used (*scatti*) at the counter after the call.

When making a call in Palermo always use the area code 091. For international calls dial 00 plus the country's code: 44 for the UK, 1 for the USA and Canada, 61 for Australia, 64 for New Zealand, 353 for Ireland. The international code for Italy is 39 and dial the full area code even when making an international call, for example, when calling Palermo from the UK, dial 00 39 092, followed by the number you want.

Useful numbers: International Directory Enquiries (🛈 176) provides phone numbers outside of Italy; operator Assistance is 🛈 170. Calls to both these numbers are subject to a charge.

Phonecards (*schede telefoniche*) are available in various euro denominations and are sold in CIT offices, post offices and tobacconists (sign with a white 'T' on a black background). Telephone boxes may be operated by telephone cards or by telephone credit cards.

### Post

The postal service can be unreliable and postcards home can take several weeks to arrive. You can buy stamps at *tabacci* (tobacconists) or at post offices. If you pay for *posta prioritaria* (priority post) your letters and cards should reach their destination more promptly.

## ELECTRICITY

The voltage is 220v 50 Hz; the sockets are for two round pin plugs. It is advisable to take an adapter for computers, hairdryers and shavers.

## TRAVELLERS WITH DISABILITIES

Many historic monuments are not equipped with lifts or wheelchair facilities. For information in Italy on which monuments are accessible by those with disabilities, contact Associazione Italiana Assistenza Spastici ⊘ Via Vitadini 3, Milano. ① 02.58.320.088; or Consorzio Cooperative Integrate ⊘ Via di Torricola 87, Rome ① 06.712.9011. ⑥ 06.712.90125.

Information in English on hotels, restaurants, museums and monuments is available at ⓦ www.italiapertutti.it.
For detailed information before you travel, contact the Royal Association for Disability and Rehabilitation (RADAR) ⊘ 12 City Forum, 250 City Road, London EC1V 8AF. ① 020 7250 3222. ⑥ 020.7250.0212. ⓦ www.radar.org.uk; radar@radar.org.uk.

## TOURIST INFORMATION
### Tourist office
**AAPIT** ① 091. 583. 847 ⓦ www.palermotourism.com

### Overseas Tourist Offices
**Italian State Tourist Office** ⊘ 1 Princes Street, London W1R 8AY, UK. ① (020) 7408 1254. ⓦ www.piuitalia2000.it
**Italian Government Tourist Board** ⊘ 630 Fifth Ave, Suite 1565, New York, NY 10111, USA. ① (212) 245 5618.
**Italian Government Tourist Board** ⊘ 175 Bloor Street East, Suite 907, South Tower, Toronto, ON M4W 3R8, Canada. ① (416) 925 4882.
**Italian Government Tourist Office** ⊘ 44 Market St, Level 6, Sydney NSW 2000, Australia. ① (02) 9262 1666.
ⓦ www.italiantourism.com.au
**Italian Tourist Office** ⊘ Italian Embassy, 34–38 Grant Road, Thorndon, Wellington, NZ. ① (04) 4947 173.

## Useful phrases

Although English is spoken in many tourist locations in Palermo, these words and phrases may come in handy. See also the phrases for specific situations in other parts of this book.

| English | Italian | *Approx. pronunciation* |
|---|---|---|
| **BASICS** | | |
| Yes | Si | *See* |
| No | Noh | *Noh* |
| Please | Per favore | *Perr fahvawreh* |
| Thank you | Grazie | *Grahtsyeh* |
| Hello | Salve | *Sahlveh* |
| Goodbye | Arrivederci | *Arreevehderrchee* |
| Excuse me | Chiedo scusa | *Kyehdaw skooza* |
| Sorry | Scusi | *Skoozee* |
| That's okay | Va bene | *Vah behneh* |
| To | A | *Ah* |
| From | Da | *Dah* |
| I don't speak Italian | Non parlo italiano | *Nawn parrlaw itahlyahnaw* |
| Do you speak English? | Parla inglese? | *Parrla eenglehzeh?* |
| Good morning | Buon giorno | *Booawn geeyawrnaw* |
| Good afternoon | Buon pomeriggio | *Booawn pawmehreehdjaw* |
| Good evening | Buona sera | *Booawnah sehrah* |
| Goodnight | Buona notte | *Booawnah nawtteh* |
| My name is ... | Mi chiamo ... | *Mee kyahmaw ...* |
| **DAYS & TIMES** | | |
| Monday | Lunedì | *Loonehdee* |
| Tuesday | Martedì | *Marrtehdee* |
| Wednesday | Mercoledì | *Merrcawlehdee* |
| Thursday | Giovedì | *Jawvehdee* |
| Friday | Venerdì | *Venerrdee* |
| Saturday | Sabato | *Sahbahtaw* |
| Sunday | Domenica | *Dawmehneeca* |
| Morning | Mattino | *Mahtteenaw* |
| Afternoon | Pomeriggio | *Pawmehreedjaw* |
| Evening | Sera | *Sehra* |
| Night | Notte | *Notteh* |
| Yesterday | Ieri | *Yeree* |

| English | Italian | Approx. pronunciation |
| --- | --- | --- |
| **Today** | Oggi | *Odjee* |
| **Tomorrow** | Domani | *Dawmahnee* |
| **What time is it?** | Che ore sono? | *Keh awreh sawnaw?* |
| **It is …** | Sono le … | *Sawnaw leh …* |
| **09.00** | Nove | *Noveh* |
| **Midday** | Mezzogiorno | *Metsawjorrnaw* |
| **Midnight** | Mezzanotte | *Metsanotteh* |

## NUMBERS

| | | |
| --- | --- | --- |
| **One** | Uno | *Oonaw* |
| **Two** | Due | *Dweh* |
| **Three** | Tre | *Treh* |
| **Four** | Quattro | *Kwahttraw* |
| **Five** | Cinque | *Cheenkweh* |
| **Six** | Sei | *Say* |
| **Seven** | Sette | *Setteh* |
| **Eight** | Otto | *Ottaw* |
| **Nine** | Nove | *Noveh* |
| **Ten** | Dieci | *Dyehchee* |
| **Eleven** | Undici | *Oondeechee* |
| **Twelve** | Dodici | *Dawdeechee* |
| **Twenty** | Venti | *Ventee* |
| **Fifty** | Cinquanta | *Cheenkwahnta* |
| **One hundred** | Cento | *Chentaw* |

## MONEY

| | | |
| --- | --- | --- |
| **I would like to change these traveller's cheques/this currency** | Vorrei cambiare questi assegni turistici/ questa valuta | *Vawrray cahmbyahreh kwestee assenee tooree-steechee/kwesta vahloota* |
| **Where is the nearest ATM?** | Dov'è il bancomat più vicino? | *Dawveh eel bankomaht pyoo veecheenaw?* |
| **Do you accept credit cards?** | Accettate carte di credito? | *Achetahteh kahrrteh dee krehdeehtaw?* |

## SIGNS & NOTICES

| | | |
| --- | --- | --- |
| **Airport** | Aeroporto | *Ahaerrhawpawrrtaw* |
| **Rail station** | Stazione ferroviaria | *Stahtsyawneh ferrawvyarya* |
| **Platform** | Binario | *Binahriaw* |
| **Smoking/non-smoking** | Per fumatori/ non fumatori | *Perr foomahtawree/ non foomahtawree* |
| **Toilets** | Bagni | *Banyee* |
| **Ladies/Gentlemen** | Signore/Signori | *Seenyawreh/Seenyawree* |
| **Subway** | Metropolitana | *Metrawpawleetahna* |

# Emergencies

## EMERGENCY NUMBERS

General emergencies ☎ 113

Police ☎ 112

Road accident ☎ 116 or 091.656.9511

Fire brigade ☎ 115

Ambulance ☎ 118

Lost property or theft ☎ 113 or 091.210.324.

The civil police force in Palermo that assists tourists is the *polizia*, based at the *questura* (police station).

## HEALTH

If you do become ill, need a dentist or are involved in an accident, ask a pharmacist to recommend a doctor or consult the local *Pagine Gialle* or Yellow Pages under *Azienda Unita Sanitaria Locale* or *Unita Sanitaria Locale Pronto Soccorso* or phone ☎ 113 and ask for *ospedale* or *ambulanza*. Hospitals in Palermo have English-speaking doctors, but the standards of healthcare are not as high as on mainland Italy. If you require emergency treatment, head to the casualty department (*pronto soccorso*) of the hospital (*ospedale*). EU citizens are entitled to free emergency medical treatment if they hold an EHIC (European Health Insurance Card). In the UK application forms for the EHIC can be obtained in post offices or by applying online (ⓦ www.ehic.org.uk).

All pharmacies (*farmacia*) hold lists of those open at night and on Sundays.

## CONSULATES & EMBASSIES

**UK Consulate** Via Cavour 117. 091.326.412.
**United States Consulate** Via Vaccarini 1. 091.305.857.

Other embassies and consulates are located on mainland Italy in
Rome, including:
**Australia Embassy** Via Allessandria 215, Rome. 06.852.721.
**Canadian Embassy** Via Zara 30, Rome. 06.445.5981
**Republic of Ireland Embassy** Piazza di Campitelli 3, Rome.
06.697.9121;
**New Zealand Embassy** Via Zara 26, Rome. 06.440.2928.
**South Africa** Via Tanaro 14, Rome. 06.852.541

---

### EMERGENCY PHRASES

**Help!** Aiuto!  *Ahyootaw!*   **Fire!** Al fuoco! *Ahl fooawcaw!*
**Stop!** Ferma! *Fairmah!*

**Call an ambulance/a doctor/the police/the fire service!**
Chiamate un'ambulanza/un medico/la polizia/i pompieri!
*Kyahmahteh oon ahmboolahntsa/ oon mehdeecaw/la*
*pawleetsya/ee pompee-ehree!*

ACKNOWLEDGEMENTS & FEEDBACK

The publishers would like to thank the folllowing for supplying their copyright photographs for this book:

Caroline Jones: all images except
A1 pix: pages 21, 40, 90, 109 and 117.
Centrale Palace Hotel: page 39.
Luigi Nifosi: pages 9, 29, 59, 79 and 126.
ENIT: pages 24 and 132.

Copy editor: Deborah Parker
Proofreader: Stuart McLaren

## Send your thoughts to
# books@thomascook.com

- **Found a great bar, club, shop or must-see sight that we don't feature?**
- **Like to tip us off about any information that needs a little updating?**
- **Want to tell us what you love about this handy little guidebook and more importantly how we can make it even handier?**

Then here's your chance to tell all! Send us ideas, discoveries and recommendations today and then look out for your valuable input in the next edition of this title. As an extra 'thank you' from Thomas Cook Publishing, you'll be automatically entered into our exciting monthly prize draw.

Email the above address (stating the title) or write to:
CitySpots Project Editor, Thomas Cook Publishing, PO Box 227, Unit 15/16, Coningsby Road, Peterborough PE3 8SB, UK.